East Cranberry Lake bathhouse in 1936.

Following page:
View from Bowman Bay.

TWO HANDS AND A SHOVEL

An illustrated exploration of the work
of the Civilian Conservation Corps
at Deception Pass State Park

Jack Hartt and Sam Wotipka, Editors

TWO HANDS AND A SHOVEL

An illustrated exploration of the work
of the Civilian Conservation Corps
at Deception Pass State Park

Copyright © 2013 by Jack Hartt and Sam Wotipka, Editors

All rights reserved. This book shall not be reproduced in whole or in part by any means, electrical or mechanical, without the prior written permission from the editors.

November 2013 edition

The publication of this book is made possible by a grant from the
Deception Pass Park Foundation.

All monies raised from sales of this book beyond the cost of production go to the Deception Pass Park Foundation, whose mission is to protect the park and educate visitors about its resources.

Your support of the Deception Pass Park Foundation helps them continue their support of this park. Visit their website at www.deceptionpassfoundation.org.

DEDICATION

One former Civilian Conservation Corps worker
stands out for his spirit of generosity
in sharing stories about the CCC,
sharing his love of this land,
and sharing abundantly of his personal resources
to make Deception Pass State Park,
Anacortes, Fidalgo Island, and Skagit County
such great places
to live and work.

John Tursi, this book is dedicated to you.

CONTENTS

Dedication	i
Contents	iii
Foreword	v
Acknowledgements	vii
Preface	xi
Prologue	1

Cornet Bay Camp

Cornet Bay	8
East Cranberry Lake	34
Old Entrance	64
North Beach	78
Highway 20, South Side	86

Rosario Camp

Rosario Camp	106
Rosario Beach	118
Reservation Bay	138
Highway 20, North Side	174

Other Park Features

Infrastructure	198
Roads	218
Trails	228
Tables	262
Camp Life	272
Park Scenery	292
Epilogue	316
Since the CCC	320
For Further Information	326
About the Editors	328

FOREWORD

Like many of the young Civilian Conservation Corps (CCC) enrollees who served at Deception Pass during the Great Depression, I knew almost nothing of this area when I first arrived here. It was the summer of 2011. I had recently graduated from college and was working in Corvallis, Oregon when I became aware of AmeriCorps, a national service organization based largely on the model of the CCC. I did a bit of research and decided that spending a year or two doing poorly paid work to help others might be preferable to immediately joining the nine-to-five working world. Through an online database of openings, I quickly applied for several positions throughout the country including one at Deception Pass. A few weeks later I had a phone interview with Jack that lasted such a short period of time that I immediately figured I had been passed over. The next day, he called to offer me the job.

At the crack of dawn on a clear September morning, I loaded up my truck and began heading north on Highway 101 towards Whidbey Island, a place that I had to find on a map despite having lived in the Pacific Northwest my whole life. I was taking 101 because I was driving a vehicle 11 years older than myself, a powder blue 1978 Datsun pickup that made up for whatever it lacked in speed and safety with a certain vintage charm. Never before having ventured far from the I-5 corridor in Washington, I was unaware that 101 splits in two near Aberdeen with the eastern arm being far more direct. I took the other. I was one hundred miles north and nearly to Forks by the time I realized my error.

I rolled into the ferry terminal at Port Townsend around 5:30, just in time to watch a half-full ship floating away. No worries, the next ferry was leaving at 6:45 and after nearly nine hours on the road the Datsun needed some time to cool off anyway. I purchased my fare and went for a walk in search of dinner, leaving my truck, piled high and sagging under the weight of all my worldly possessions, steaming in the waiting lane.

I returned just as the line was beginning to move and turned the key in the ignition. Nothing. The cars behind me pulled around and boarded the ferry as I fruitlessly fumbled beneath the hood. An hour or so later, as daylight was beginning to fade, I finally located a loose wire and, covered in engine grease, pulled onto the final ferry of the day.

By the time I made it to the park, it was nearly 11 p.m. and there was no one around to give me the key to my house. I spent my first night at Deception Pass camping in site 98, waking early enough to avoid paying.

Aside from my initial ignorance of this area and the fact that I traveled to Whidbey Island on a ferry, the similarities between my own circumstances and those of the CCC enrollees who worked at here are scant. John Tursi, the Corps member to whom this book is dedicated, once told me the story of how he ended up at Deception Pass. Orphaned, hungry and homeless on the streets of Brooklyn at age fourteen during the Great Depression, John set off to West Virginia in search of work. He spent several months hitchhiking and wandering through the countryside on foot but was unable to find anyone willing to hire a fourteen-year-old kid. By the time he made his way back to New York, he had gangrene in his foot from weeks of walking in the same socks and claims he would have had his leg amputated had he returned the next day to the hospital where he was diagnosed. At sixteen, he lied about his age to a police sergeant and was enrolled in the CCC.

John was put on a train with dozens of other destitute young men from New York. "Anacortes, Washington" was written on the side of the car. Few of the enrollees, many of whom were dropouts or petty criminals, had ever traveled outside of New York and most of them assumed that there had been a typo and they were actually headed to Anaconda, an airfield outside of Washington, D.C. Five days later they arrived at the train station in Anacortes where they were loaded into army trucks leftover from World War I and driven to Yokeko Point. The Deception Pass Bridge had not yet been built and they were shuttled across the pass to the northern tip of Whidbey Island on a rickety five-car ferry. The rest, as they say, is history.

As I began working at Deception Pass, I quickly realized the incredible debt owed to the CCC members who worked for little more than food and a roof over their heads to develop this magnificent park. Evidence of their skills, perseverance and commitment are ubiquitous here. I believe that there is a great amount of enduring wisdom and knowledge that can be gleaned from John's story and the story of the millions of other men like him who served in the CCC across this nation. During my time at Deception Pass, I have tried my best to ensure that their accomplishments are not lost and their stories are not forgotten. This book, I hope, will help.

On a personal level, I am particularly grateful for the success of the CCC which proved the value of national service and paved the way for the creation of AmeriCorps in 1993. I will always feel a special kinship with the men pictured in this book. Helping to protect and preserve their legacy has been among the most rewarding experiences of my life.

Sam Wotipka
Whidbey Island, 2013

ACKNOWLEDGEMENTS

No book like this can be written without the help of many.

The photographers of the 1930s who took the photos are to be commended for their work, sometimes catching Corps members hard at work, sometimes having members pose for a picture, sometimes capturing an unplanned scene that has endearing and enduring value.

Sam Wotipka, serving as an AmeriCorps member at Deception Pass State Park, sparked the idea for this book. He has taken a hands-on approach to restoring CCC facilities around the park, re-invigorating the CCC museum at Bowman Bay, organizing maintenance parties of CCC buildings and signs, developing interpretive displays at Cornet Bay, giving programs about the park history, and developing photographs from some of those printed here for display around the park.

It was Sam who recognized that Deception Pass State Park had an extensive photographic record of the productive CCC segment of park history, photos that were languishing unseen in park files and databases. He began to bring them to light with a handful of prints displayed at the Cornet Bay Retreat Center.

With so much more available, he suggested that a portfolio or book could be published showcasing these photos. I caught the spark, and also realized that we had CCC stories and personal histories that deserved a wider hearing as well.

And as the manager of this iconic and beloved park, I have always felt a duty to make sure that decisions about the park are based on the dimension of long term thinking, incorporating the heritage of our past with the wisdom of the future as seen in the eyes of our grandchildren and their grandchildren. Capturing the insights and dreams of the CCC era as it affected and directed the development of Deception Pass State Park seemed like an obviously appropriate endeavor.

The board members of the Deception Pass Park Foundation have shown an unending desire to share the joys and values of Deception Pass with the world. Their support and funding of this project is just another example of their dedication to giving and sharing their love of this place. The funds they raise are made possible by every individual who contributes to their cause: the protection and interpretation of Deception Pass State Park. Board members include Liz Merriman, President; Barry Wenaas, Vice President; Steve Young; George Churchill; Matt Klope; Brian Shelly; Estelle Johnson; and Barb Shaw.

We are grateful to so many of our park neighbors and friends who have assisted with the ongoing work of maintaining and restoring park facilities. The Skagit-Whatcom-Island Trail Maintaining Organization (SWITMO) has volunteered thousands of hours in getting quality cedar logs, hand-splitting shakes, and wheelbarrowing these to roofs around the park for installation, to say nothing of the miles of trails they have built and also restored.

HDR Engineering of Seattle, led by Lex Palmer and Martha Weiss, and assisted by Steven Starlund and Gunnar Christiansen of Washington State Parks, have helped rebuild and maintain shelters as well.

Harrison Goodall of Whidbey Island deserves special mention for encouraging and personally participating in preservation and restoration work throughout the park.

Dozens of Boy Scout troops, church groups, local Lions Clubs, and other volunteer organizations have helped with building maintenance and other related projects throughout the years.

Nearby Whidbey Island Naval Air Station active duty groups have also assisted throughout the park in various restoration projects.

Recently, the Retired Chief Petty Officers Association of Whidbey Island has volunteered many hours of hard labor to restore various park features. A special thanks to Bud Betz for organizing this group and for his dedication to doing things right, working hard, and having fun.

Julian Lee, a Rosario neighbor, has rebuilt the Corps-made entrance signs at Rosario Beach, re-creating the new signs to look nearly identical to the originals. He is currently at work on more projects around the park.

Ted Lagreid of eastern Washington, whose father and grandfather were stone masons and helped build the stoves with the CCC, sponsored the reconstruction of two CCC-built rock stoves at Deception Pass.

There are so many people who have dedicated a weekend or a lifetime to helping Deception Pass State Park; I apologize for not naming every one of you. You all deserve honor and recognition for the commendable work you have done to carry on the tradition of the CCC and preserve these landmarks for others to enjoy.

Mark Lunz, Marvin Wold, and Dan Dillard, our maintenance staff at the park in 2004, were the primary creators of the base of the CCC statue at Bowman Bay. Take a look at the quality of rockwork that went into that base. Mark's father was a Corps member, so he feels a special connection with the work of the CCC. Our maintenance team, assisted by Wayne Todd Harris and various park rangers, continues to work on CCC structures or landscapes nearly every day of the year. Their sensitivity to the value and quality of their work in historical preservation while allowing ongoing use cannot be overemphasized.

The upper shelter at Bowman Bay, restored by members of the Whidbey Island Retired Chief Petty Officers and current active duty members from Naval Air Station Whidbey Island.

Other current park staff have given of themselves for years to assist in any way that they can to maintain and operate this busiest of all Washington State Parks. Rick Blank, Jeri Lancaster, Ben Shook, Jason Stapert, John Whittet, Bill Ruh, and Jim Aggergaard stand out for the effort they have put into maintaining these historic park facilities and the rest of the park. Jason Stapert and John Whittet also have the privilege and challenge of caring for two of these buildings on a daily basis, and their work is gratefully appreciated and recognized. Region Manager Eric Watilo has provided generous assistance and volunteer labor as well.

The work of previous park and region state park staff throughout the past eighty years are also honored for keeping these facilities intact for such a long time. In spite of lean budgets, competing interests, and overwhelming workloads, these structures and features have been kept functioning for all these years. Well done, park staff through the ages.

Adam Lorio assisted for many years as the park interpreter at Deception Pass, and furthered our interpretive efforts about the CCC. He spent many hours recording oral histories and preserving the records of the CCC so far as our limited resources would allow. He also helped with our

75th birthday party in 2008 for the Civilian Conservation Corps, assisted also by then-Rangers Henk Sikkenga and Devin Corcoran. Ranger Corcoran, who lived in the Bowman Bay CCC house at the time, generously opened up his house for visitors to tour.

Alex McMurry, Washington State Parks preservation specialist, contributes frequently to our discussions about the work of the CCC, and has helped financially and with sweat equity in the restoration of many of our CCC facilities.

Our thanks also to then-director of Washington State Parks, Rex Derr, for his financial and personal support of the CCC statue project, and for his warmth in congratulating the CCC members during the ceremonies of the statue dedication and 75th anniversary events.

The men and women of the CCC Alumni Chapter 5 of Seattle, with Berniece Phelps as president, were constant advocates for educating people about the work of the CCC. When their chapter retired, they gave their chapter funds to the park to further the story of the Corps.

Chapter 78 of the CCC Alumni created the momentum and collections that eventually led to the development of the interpretive center at the Bowman Bay bathhouse. Their legacy lives on for all of us.

Of course, a personal thanks to Susannah Hartt and Benjamin Hartt for putting up with umpteen requests for their thoughts about this book, and for putting up with not seeing me for hours or even days on end as the book came together.

Most of all, we must give credit to the men of the CCC, who did the work that we so admire. Most of their names are recorded only as one line in a ledger somewhere.

We know that their names are written in the work that they did—in the patterned stones, the finely-fitted woodwork, the new roadways and cleared fields, the trails and tables and waterlines and legends that they created all in a day's work.

We acknowledge our debt of gratitude for the work they accomplished in building this park, for crafting a design that still brings us to the park to be a part of this heritage of nature and culture, to enjoy our time with family and friends, and to experience the great outdoors right in our backyard.

Their work made Deception Pass State Park the iconic gem that hosts two million visitors a year—two million individuals appreciating the park features created and developed by the men of the CCC, one stone, one log, and one shovel full at a time.

Jack Hartt
Fidalgo Island, 2013

PREFACE

Times were tough. One out of four workers was unemployed. A thousand families a day gave up their homes, unable to pay the mortgages. Lines at charity soup kitchens stretched down the street for several blocks.

The newly elected president, Franklin Roosevelt, wanted to get the nation back on its feet, and its young men back in action, learning work skills while bettering the country. Within six weeks of his taking office, Roosevelt had signed the Civilian Conservation Corps into existence.

> *"It was just a means of taking care of the family.... Things were so bad, you know. Twenty five dollars a month went home to buy food for the rest of the family, and that was it at the time."*

Over three million men from around the nation aged 18 to 25 signed up over the course of the program for duty at a park, forest, or other outdoor facility. They built roads, trails, houses, and restrooms. They planted trees, fought forest fires, and protected farmland. They learned how to work, how to work with others, and how to give back to their country. They learned new skills and old traditional disciplines. They earned $30 a month, $25 of which was sent back home to their families. They were given three meals a day, a place to sleep, and the tools to do hard work.

In return, they worked hard, earned self-respect, and gained hope for the future.

This collection of photographs is shared as a tribute to the men of the Civilian Conservation Corps who built many of the most iconic features and facilities at Deception Pass State Park in the state of Washington.

The photos are from a variety of sources. The majority were taken by National Park Service personnel documenting the work of the Corps members at each location where they worked. They are published here with the purpose of honoring the stories of the men of the CCC, and recognizing and highlighting the work that they did to build our parks and rebuild our nation.

These photos are reproduced from prints of varying quality available in various historical collections. Some show fine details; some are not as sharp, or have scratches, smudge spots or other defects in the print. Some of these have been touched up a little to remove some of the defects.

The original NPS prints have numbers written on the edges, in the white space surrounding the prints, and also dates that are approximations of when the photos were taken. Some of the original prints also have typewritten or typed notes attached to them giving a little explanation or context for the photo. These edges and notes have been cropped from the photos in this book for a cleaner appearance, but explanatory notes are added under most of the pictures so that the reader can gain further understanding of the background of the photos.

For the most part, all of the NPS photos were taken in late 1933 through 1935.

Several photos are from the collection of John Tursi, gathered during his tenure at the Cornet Bay camp in 1934 and 1935. Credit is given to Mr. Tursi for the pictures attributed to him.

A handful of pictures are from other archived photos in the collections of the Washington State Parks and Recreation Commission, stored as digital archives in the Washington State archives. Most of these photos were taken around 1935 to 1936. Credit is given on each page that shares a photo from the archives. For each of these photos, the following credit applies:

> Source: State Parks and Recreation Commission, Recreation and Development, Photographs of State Parks and Park Development, 1933-1938, Washington State Archives. Original images held at the Washington State Archives, Olympia, WA.
> Digital Archives,
> http://www.digitalarchives.wa.gov

A couple photos are from other donated collections and gifts to the park, photos that were taken during the time of the CCC camps at this park. All are shared here so that they may receive a wider viewership.

Loose leaf cover of the collection of photographs taken by National Park Service photographers at Deception Pass.

The photographs are arranged primarily by geography. Each area of the park where work was done by the CCC has its own chapter. We have limited our comments about the photos to brief descriptions where necessary, letting the pictures themselves tell their story. To help the reader get oriented, the locations of the photos are indicated on a map at the beginning of each chapter. The locations of a handful of the photos cannot be precisely determined, however.

In the following pages we let photographs from the CCC era walk us through the major areas of Deception Pass State Park. Starting at Cornet Bay, we move to the east shore of Cranberry Lake, then to North Beach and West Beach, and then to the highway project on the Whidbey Island side.

Then we cross to the north side of the pass, looking at camp life at Rosario, projects at Rosario Beach, Reservation Bay, and the highway project leading from Pass Lake to the bridge at the pass.

The next section looks at the details of the infrastructure work of the crews, such as mundane features like roadways, water lines, sewer systems, tables, benches, trails, signs, and hardware. From there, we see what camp life was like; it was not always work time.

We finish by highlighting scenic views from around the park, captured by these same photographers who could not resist attempting to capture the beauty that was all around them.

Rather than show 'before and after' pictures, this book provides the 'before' only, the original historical photographs, and gives you the reader enough information to take your own 'after' picture for comparison when you visit the park. For most of these photos you will find ample clues and landmarks still remaining to help you rediscover yesterday's stories in today's scenery.

PROLOGUE

Salish peoples have lived along the shores of the Salish Sea for thousands of years. Numerous bays, beaches, and broad headlands supported large populations in this area. The tribes thrived with the abundant and diverse resources of food and useful materials for shelter and clothing.

Summarizing their lives in a few paragraphs or even a few chapters does not give their cultures the respect and honor that it truly deserves, so please review in-depth authoritative studies to gain a better understanding of the first peoples in this area.

Caucasian culture entered the area with explorers in the late eighteenth century. Manuel Quimper and Juan Carrasco explored the eastern Strait of Juan de Fuca in 1790 from the Spanish base at Nootka Sound. Their commander, Francisco Eliza, sent several other expeditions through the strait towards the Strait of Georgia and Admiralty Inlet in 1791. These expeditions named several of the geographical features of the area, including the name Fidalgo Island in honor of one of the Spanish explorers based at Nootka. They gave the name "Boca de Flon" ("Mouth of Flon") to what they thought was the mouth of a large river south of Fidalgo Island, the area of Deception Pass.

A year later Captain George Vancouver of Great Britain approached the area from the south. He sent his ship master Joseph Whidbey into a harbor that Vancouver called Port Gardner, near present-day Everett, while Vancouver sailed up Admiralty Inlet. Vancouver anchored off the west side of a waterway he noticed had a swift current.

Whidbey eventually explored enough of that waterway from the east side and the west side to prove that the land they had sailed around was an island, not part of the mainland as they had thought. Captain Vancouver named the waterway "Deception Pass," having been deceived into thinking it was a bay or river mouth. He also honored Whidbey by naming the newly discovered island to the south "Whidbey's Island."

The north shore of Deception Pass, looking westward toward the Strait of Juan de Fuca.

What may be the earliest written description of the Pass was written by Vancouver who wrote, "A very narrow and intricate channel, which for a considerable distance was not forty yards in width, and abounded in rocks above and beneath the surface of the water. These impediments in addition to the great rapidity and irregularity of the tide rendered this passage navigable only for boats or vessels of very small berthen."

These explorations led to the eventual arrival of pioneers and homesteaders throughout the region, along with diseases and cultural changes that devastated the native tribes and their ways of life.

The Deception Pass area was recognized in the middle of the nineteenth century for its potential as a location to defend against an enemy wishing to enter Puget Sound. The federal government set aside about 1700 acres of land on both sides of the Pass as a military reservation. Soldiers were stationed here during times of war. Guns on rocky promontories guarded the pass.

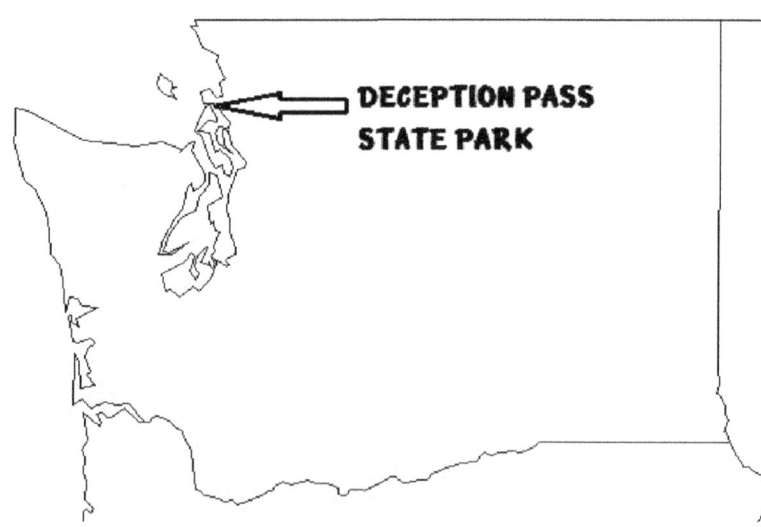

Outline map of the state of Washington, showing the location of Deception Pass State Park at the north end of Whidbey Island and the south end of Fidalgo Island. The current park boundary encompasses about six square miles scattered over all or portions of ten islands.

At West Point, a searchlight scanned the waters of the strait in order to detect enemy ships at night.

None ever came.

The nearby lands and beaches had always been popular as a park with local residents, who had held picnics on the shores of Cranberry Lake and Rosario Beach for many years in the early twentieth century. Some held rallies here to raise support for building a bridge across the pass to connect Whidbey Island with Fidalgo Island and then to the mainland.

When World War I ended, the United States no longer saw any military value to the reservation. President Harding committed the land to Washington State Parks on March 25, 1922. The local Anacortes newspaper celebrated the action a few days later and the park was dedicated that year, formally creating Deception Pass State Park, one of the earliest parks in the Washington State Park system. President Coolidge signed the official deed transfer on February 11, 1925.

Although it was now officially a state park, the newly created park had no funding, no facilities, no staff, and no plans for the future. The State Board of Park Commissioners, started in 1913 to put together a state park system, was a fledgling agency with limited resources. In 1921, the Board's activities were finally codified into law, giving the Board specific powers to manage parks. The Board was renamed the State Parks Committee.

Land acquisition for parks was one challenge; development of the parks for public use was another, while operations and maintenance was yet a third challenge. The Committee operated without much funding. Facilities development was limited and plain. It was a constant struggle to keep existing parks open and maintained.

And then in 1929, newly elected Governor Roland Hartley removed all funding from the park system, considering parks to be a frivolous waste of tax money. The park system basically closed down for four years, subjecting parks to vandalism and deterioration. As the Great Depression gripped the nation, Washington State Parks were shuttered and left undeveloped, unprotected, and mostly unused.

In 1933, a new Governor, Clarence D. Martin, gave new life to the parks. He restored some funding, allowing parks to reopen and to be repaired. A state program similar to the CCC was enacted at the state level to give 300 men a chance to help clean parks and get them ready for use. The Committee also hired William H.

Weigle to be the first State Parks Superintendent.

Difficult events at the national level would soon result in a blessing for Washington State Parks.

As the Great Depression extended its grip to all of America, almost two million men and women adopted a vagrant existence. At the same time, our nation faced the consequences of several generations of exploitation of natural resources. This economic self-interest resulted in a nation that had exhausted soil, denuded forests, and over-grazed grasslands.

Of all the crises that faced the nation, unemployment was perhaps the most pressing. Over 25 percent of the labor force was without jobs.

The newly-elected President Franklin Roosevelt wasted no time in addressing these issues.

Within six weeks of taking office, he had presented to Congress a bill for "The Relief of Unemployment Through the Performance of Useful Public Work and for Other Purposes," putting forth the Emergency Conservation Work Act, the framework for what was eventually called the Civilian Conservation Corps.

Of all the "New Deal" programs, the CCC was clearly Roosevelt's favorite. It accomplished two important goals – preservation of the nation's natural resources and its human resources.

"We are definitely in an era of building," Roosevelt said, "the best kind of building -- the building of great public projects for the benefit of the public and with the definite objective of building human happiness."

"It will conserve our precious natural resources. It will pay dividends to the present and future generations. It will make improvements in national and state domains which have been largely forgotten in the past few years of industrial development.

"More important, however, than the material gains will be the moral and spiritual value of such work. The overwhelming majority of unemployed Americans, who are now walking the streets and receiving private or public relief, would infinitely prefer to work. We can take a vast army of these unemployed out into healthful surroundings. We can eliminate to some extent at least the threat that enforced idleness brings to spiritual and moral stability. It is not a panacea for all the unemployment but it is an essential step in this emergency."

The Department of Labor was chosen to select the men; the War Department would feed, clothe, house, and transport them; the Departments of Agriculture and the Interior would select work projects, supervise the work, and manage the camps.

Originally intended for unmarried and unemployed men between the ages of 18 and 25, the program was expanded soon after to include parolees and qualified veterans, as long as they were in need of work. By July of 1933, more than 300,000 men had been brought into the program.

> *"The President's objective in all this work is to build men as well as forests."*
> — John H. Markham, General Superintendent of State CCC Camps

When President Roosevelt offered the CCC program as a source of park development funding and workers, the Washington State Parks Committee welcomed the opportunity gratefully.

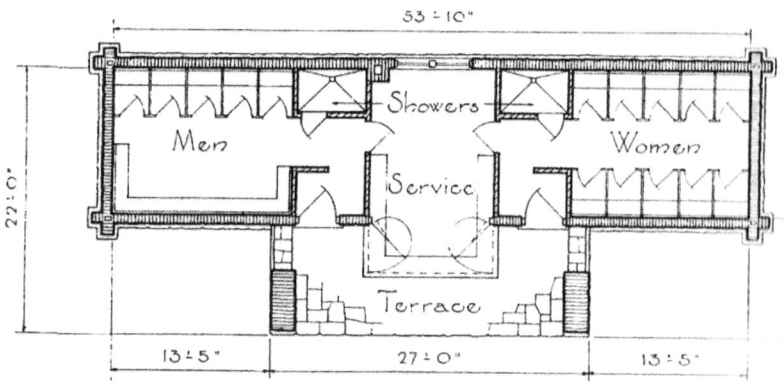

Overhead view of the design of the bathhouse at East Cranberry Lake. Drawing from Patterns from the Golden Age of Rustic Design *by Albert Good.*

Eleven camps were planned for the state. Deception Pass State Park would receive two of these camps, one on each side of the pass.

With no staff to assist the program, State Parks allowed the National Park Service to take the lead in designing the development of the new state park at Deception Pass, and to organize the CCC crews that would do the work.

With such a dramatic impact coming to parks around the nation, the National Park Service developed design standards to guide the work, plans which were conceptual in nature, allowing specific adaptations depending on the individual park's environment. A non-intrusive ethic for buildings and structures had begun to grow in the late nineteenth century. The style was highly adaptable, and through the use of native materials could incorporate features from local forms or indigenous architecture.

The principles and practices were both practical and aesthetic. They came from commitments to providing stewardship for park scenery, preserving parks as inviolate places, and blending construction with natural conditions. Each park was therefore encouraged to experiment, innovate, and refine in a never ending search for sensible, simple, and pragmatic solutions that followed function on one hand and nature on the other.

Some called it naturalistic design, or "rustic design." Native materials were used when available. Silhouettes were low, emphasizing horizontal planes. Straight lines and right angles were avoided where possible, emphasizing curving lines, random patterns, and overall appearances harmonious with the surrounding landscapes.

The architecture they employed was a function of the era, and ideally suited to the conditions of a depressed economy and widespread unemployment. Labor intensive, this rustic architecture employed the combined efforts of many men, skilled and unskilled, in planning, preparing, and building. Yet it was also economical in that it employed the use of natural and native materials, certainly what was locally abundant, for little or no cost.

The essence of this design style is summarized by Arno B. Cammerer, Director of the National Park Service in a foreword he wrote in 1935:

> "In any area in which the preservation of the beauty of Nature is a primary purpose, every modification of the natural landscape, whether it be by construction of a road or erection of a shelter, is an intrusion. A basic objective of those who are entrusted with development of such areas for the human uses for which they are established, is...to hold these intrusions to a minimum and to design them that, besides being attractive to look upon, they appear to belong to and be a part of their settings."

The architecture of the buildings required strict adherence to the principles of the design guidelines, with the freedom that each specific location suggested through topography and native materials. Floor plans were therefore neither standard nor original, but a blending of both. Ellsworth Storey designed several of the buildings at Deception Pass. Another architect, Mr. R. Koepf, created the designs for the beach shelters at Rosario and Bowman Bay, and the bathhouse at Cranberry Lake.

The plans they developed called for the park activities to be focused at the beaches: North Beach in particular, but also Cornet Bay, the east end of Cranberry Lake, Rosario Beach, and Reservation Bay (named because of the military reservation; today called Bowman Bay after an early pioneer family on Fidalgo Island). Roads would connect Oak Harbor to Cornet Bay, and then span out to North Beach and Cranberry Lake.

To make these projects happen, two camps were planned: one on the south side, at Cornet Bay, and one on the north side, near Rosario Beach. Both camps were operational before the end of 1933. For the rest of the decade, CCC members labored to create the recreational landscape we now enjoy at Deception Pass State Park. Under the supervision of local experienced men, the CCC boys used little more than their hands and primitive tools to turn raw natural materials into durable structures appropriate for the landscape.

Cornet Bay was the site of a former Salish tribal camp. At the head of the bay, the area was heavily forested with dense and large trees, but with fairly level ground leading down to the edge of the water. From this camp the workers could also focus on the already-popular east side of Cranberry Lake and North Beach, as well as trails leading to dramatic park attractions such as West Beach, Goose Rock, and Hoypus Point.

On the north side of the pass, a camp was built in a sloping field between Cougar Gap and Rosario Beach. From here, the crews would build a water system to serve Rosario and Reservation Bay, a caretaker house at Reservation Bay, several shelters and restrooms, and miles of roads and trails.

Another effort from President Roosevelt to get the economy jump started was a program called the Works Progress Administration (renamed the Work Projects Administration in 1939), committed to building the nation's infrastructure of highways, dams, and other critical components. Funding was found through this program to finally help build a bridge connecting Whidbey and Fidalgo Islands, giving direct vehicle access to Whidbey Island for the first time.

O. R. Elwell of the Washington Department of Highways (now the Department of Transportation) engineered the bridge. The Puget Construction Company of Seattle built the bridge, with steel fabrication by the Wallace Bridge and Structural Steel Company of Seattle.

But there were no roads leading to the bridge. With the CCC camps in place on both sides of the pass, the CCC members were the logical choice to help build the new highway approaches through the park.

The north side camp had the bigger challenge. Solid rock bluffs above Pass Lake made that section difficult, but not even close to the difficulty of having to blast through rock on heavily forested and precipitously steep slopes at the north end of the pass itself. The Cornet Bay camp had somewhat easier terrain, but also had to blast through a hill of rock near the pass, and build an underpass for the park road going to North Beach under the new highway.

Both crews also built the guard rails alongside the new highway, making distinctive and

When I became assistant leader I got six dollars a month more, and I had that all to myself. And that was really something in those days.

— Ed Cole, enrollee

attractive rock stanchions holding up thick logs to channel traffic along the roadway and protect vehicles from the vertical slopes at the highway's edge.

The two camps were home to hundreds of young men from 1933 to 1942. These hungry, jobless, and occasionally homeless men lived here, earning enough money to keep their families back home alive, and eventually going back home themselves with enough experience and expertise to be productive members of a growing economy.

They experienced discipline, they learned work skills, and they were encouraged to take on additional responsibilities at camp. Many used this opportunity to learn skills that they could then use in a career of their own. Enrollees also worked for promotions to assistant leaders or to be leaders themselves. In these jobs they served as cooks, stewards, storekeepers, clerks, clerical staff, and other special positions. With the added responsibility came increased pay, pay that they could save or spend as they wished.

By working here, they also developed the core facilities of a new state park that would soon become one of the most popular attractions in all of Washington State. The facilities they built became the infrastructure of a park that now hosts millions of visitors each year.

Park rangers now reside in the caretaker cabins built by the CCC, travel roads built by the CCC to care for restrooms and shelters built by the CCC, and hike several miles of trails built by the CCC. Visitors have weddings in CCC shelters, swim at a CCC-developed beach, refresh themselves in CCC-built restrooms, hike from Bowman Bay to the lighthouse or up to Goose Rock on CCC-made trails, and drink from faucets bringing water through CCC-installed pipe lines.

Many of the facilities built here by the Corps remain as useful and popular as when they were first constructed. Some have been modified to serve other purposes, and just one has been lost from neglect or from not understanding the historical value of the structure.

Wherever you go in Deception Pass you will see the evidence of the CCC. Their structures were built to fit the environment, to look like they belong here. Most of what they built was created from locally available materials: wood and stone.

Marvel at the quality of their construction: from the precise angles in joining logs in buildings, to the various patterns incorporated into stonework, to the detailed design work in a door handle or window frame.

These men worked with little more than their hands and hand tools. Beyond that they had limited resources. They found a way to get things done instead with different currencies: that of dedication, team work, hard work, and creativity.

Yes, the legacy of the Civilian Conservation Corps lives on, beloved every day by us visitors from a more "modern" time. The work that they did still frames the landscapes that fill the lenses of our cameras and the visions of our minds.

CCC Camps in Washington State Parks:
  Beacon Rock
  Deception Pass
  Ginkgo
  Lewis and Clark
  Millersylvania
  Moran
  Mount Spokane
  Rainbow Falls
  Riverside
  Saltwater
  Twanoh

WPA projects in Washington State Parks:
  Bridle Trails
  Dry Falls
  Illahee
  Kitsap Memorial
  Lake Sylvia
  Larrabee
  Lewis and Clark Trail
  Sacajawea
  Schafer
  Sequim Bay

CORNET BAY

Cornet Bay hides just inside Deception Pass, on the southern shore. The shores of the bay sheltered encampments of Swinomish tribal peoples for centuries. Caucasians homesteaded the bay in the mid-1800s, creating openings in the forest and leaving behind colorful and questionable stories of their lives on the frontier.

Eventually, a roadway from Oak Harbor followed the shores of the bay to Hoypus Point, where a ferry provided the only automobile service connecting the north end of Whidbey Island with the mainland.

In the early twentieth century, the woods at the head of the bay were heavily forested, similar to the old growth forests on the sides of Goose Rock. The trees soared to 200 feet, with diameters of some of the trees well over five feet thick.

Protected from timber harvesting because it was part of the military reservation, the newly created Deception Pass State Park had a handful of trails lacing through these trees but little else. The head of Cornet Bay provided a fairly flat bowl facing the water, separate from the handful of homes that had sprung up elsewhere along the bay.

It was this bay where Civilian Conservation Corps leaders decided to establish the first camp for Deception Pass. Called SP-3, because it was the third camp established in a Washington State Park, the military numbered the camp as 266 Company of the C. C. C.

The first camp had to start with nothing but a dense forest along the shore of the bay. Their first job was removing hundreds of large Douglas fir and other evergreen trees, then removing the stumps, leveling the ground, and developing the outline of a camp.

At the same time they needed to set up tent shelters for residency, and buildings for cooking meals and storing tools and other materials.

This first group, from Delaware, arrived in late 1933, and apparently left early, unable to handle the difficult work and distressing wet winter conditions of the Pacific Northwest. The rainfall that winter was far more than the local average, turning the fields to mud.

The next group, from New York and New Jersey, took their place a few months later in 1934. In this second camp were convicts out of prison, parolees on probation, three lawyers, a concert violinist, a classic guitarist, and a sixteen year old boy named John Tursi.

Over the years, because of crews like these, buildings grew and were refined; the camp became formalized and more comfortable. Park structures took shape, and a new highway opened up the island.

This chapter illustrates the establishment of the camp and the development of the many facilities that would become the center of operations for Camp Deception, SP-3, Company 266, working throughout all of Deception Pass State Park south of the pass itself.

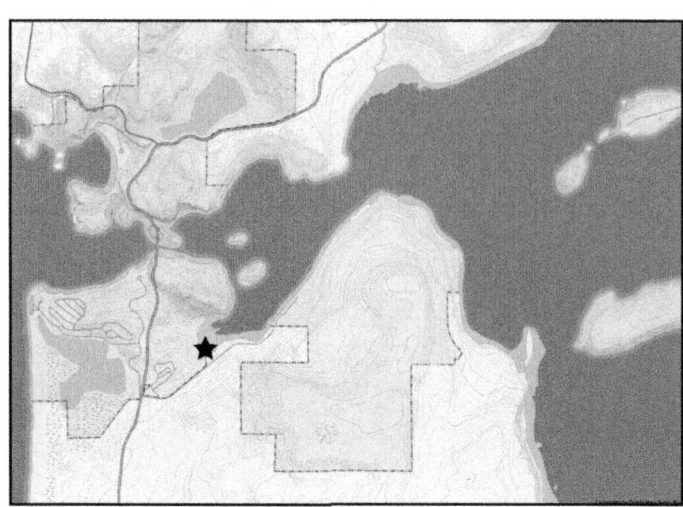

Cornet Bay

Above:
Heavy blasting cleared the thick field of stumps left behind after cutting the forest for the new camp. Over one half-ton of powder was used in just one afternoon as part of the process of clearing the stumps. Although supervised by men experienced in using dynamite, the charges were placed and fired by the young CCC enrollees as part of the education and experience of being in the CCC. The waters of Cornet Bay can be seen beyond the explosive blast in this view looking northeast.

Below:
CCC enrollees clearing the fields of the camp area by burning the stumps and other debris. The fires would burn for weeks on end.

Cornet Bay

Above:
Two CCC members fanning the flames of a stump pile to help the wet and green wood to burn better.

View is facing north, close to the bay, with Goose Rock in the background.

Right:
Splitting the rounds cut from trees as the field is cleared at Cornet Bay. The firewood will be used in the stoves of the mess hall.

Cornet Bay

Above:
Mess hall being framed in the distance, near the site of the current lodge and dining hall for the Cornet Bay Retreat Center. Goose Rock rises in the distance.

Below:
Many hands make clearing and grubbing for tent platforms an easier task. View is facing northeast, not far from the shoreline of the bay.

Cornet Bay

Above:
Framing the root house. This building was to be used as the tool house for the Cornet Bay Recreation Area when the camp was removed. It no longer exists.

Right:
Tent pads are nearly done, as a large debris pile burns near the water's edge. View looking north from the main field area.

Cornet Bay

Above:
Two different styles of tents are up. The trees in the background show full foliage, indicating that this is summer of the first year. But the ground still looks muddy after the long winter of rain. The tents are sitting directly on the mud at this point.

Below:
These tents appear to be the same ones seen above, as seen from a different angle.

Cornet Bay

Above:
The mess hall is now complete; the stumps remain to be burned, and smoke can be seen rising near the water's edge.

Below:
Workers notch logs in preparation for building a tool shed. Compare the notches seen here with the final product in the picture on the next page. In the background, the size of the trees that were felled here can be seen, as enrollees cut those into large rounds for creating lumber.

Cornet Bay

Cornet Bay, as seen from near the summit of Goose Rock. Camp SP-3 can be seen in the opening near the water's edge, with tents lined up. Smoke rises from slash piles that continue to burn.

View looking south down Whidbey Island. Goose Rock is the highest point on Whidbey Island.

Cornet Bay

Above:
Camp entrance stockade fence under construction.

Below:
The completed stockade in place. View looking through the gate towards the flagpole in the center of the grounds.

Sign on the gate reads:
          266-CO
          C.C.C.

This camp was the 266th CCC camp established in the nation.

Cornet Bay

Above:
Al Davis, foreman of the camp in 1934, stands on the left at the entrance in front of the new stockade fence. The simple quality of the fence shows that it was put up quickly, without the design and appearance standards that will appear in CCC work in the near future.

Below:
The parting. Some of the young men going home, some remaining for a second tour of duty.

Picture taken in the morning, looking northeast.

Cornet Bay

Above:
The completed tool shed. The details of craftsmanship were taught by local expert craftsmen, who shared their skills with the young Corps members to enable the crews to create quality facilities.

Below:
The tool shed gets used as CCC men get busy. A stack of shakes is ready on the left for building a roof. Notice the front wheel of the wheel barrow — all metal. This building cannot be found today. It may have been a temporary structure for the CCC camp use only.

Cornet Bay

Above:
A CCC worker is high in a tree, removing dead limbs to make the camp safer on a windy day.

Right:
Inset picture shows the worker more clearly, holding onto a branch high in the tree on the left side of the photo above.

Branches like this were called 'widow-makers' for the problems they caused when they would break off unexpectedly high above anyone below. The photo also gives a dramatic view of the scale of trees in the Pacific Northwest.

Cornet Bay

Above:
The wooden framed mess hall stands completed on the left. Tents served as shelter for the first crew of workers at Cornet Bay. Construction material on the right-hand side of the picture waits to be used. The rainfall during the winter of 1933-1934 turned the field to thick mud. Most of the CCC enrollees abandoned the camp that first winter, going back to their homes in Delaware.

Below:
Group picture of a full camp, SP-3, 266 Company, CCC. The field is muddy after the long winter.

"Tents were erected on the hillside and rain was really coming down, ditches had to be dug around the tents, so the water would run down into our future parade grounds, that became a mud hole. Our latrine consisted of a log on the side of a ditch. Cranberry Lake made a wonderful bathhouse, but very cold."

—Enrollee, Camp Deception Pass

Cornet Bay

Above:
The CCC crew stops for a photo while working on clearing stumps and building tent frame foundations.

Looking towards the mess hall, north of the main field.

Right:
Tent frames are being built for more permanent shelter. Fires are burning in the background to help clear the land.

View north to Cornet Bay and Goose Rock

Cornet Bay

Above:
The view down Company Street, looking north. The tents are more comfortable now, having wooden bases.

In the foreground, Lt. G. W. Bostain, Camp Commander, examines forestry exhibits in the educational display of the camp.

In August 1933, the *Farm Bureau News* described the Cornet Bay camp: "On the right, lining Delaware Avenue, are forty board-floored tents, each with a heating stove and equipped to house from four to six men. The two end tents are the Post Exchange, or 'canteen,' and the hospital tent. At the far end of Delaware Avenue is the new bath house."

Cornet Bay

Above:
Another crew of enrollees arrives at camp. The camp itself is starting to look developed and welcoming. Note that the tents are gone, replaced by bunkhouses with real roofs. It took quite some time to make the camp fully functional and relatively comfortable for the workers.

Below:
Camp supplies arrive, which are quickly unloaded by crew members.

The two views almost match up side to side for a panoramic view of the camp.

Cornet Bay

Above:
New enrollees unload their personal belongings and begin to meet each other. Commanding officers in the foreground wait to address them and begin the process of training new recruits. Camps were run with military protocol and discipline.

Below:
Several members holding ropes on the flagpole to keep it in place while another worker loosens the bolts to allow the flagpole to be lowered for maintenance.

Cornet Bay

Above:
Supervised play on a Saturday morning. Several new details of ongoing camp improvements can be seen in the picture. The flagpole is now complete and has landscaping.

Below:
A full camp of CCC workers at Camp Deception, Cornet Bay.

Camp SP-3, 266 Co.

25

Cornet Bay

Above:
Another full camp of CCC workers at Camp Deception.

Below:
Lt. G. W. Bostain, United States Navy, Camp Commander, looking over a big fir stump in the camp area, early in the camp's beginnings.

Cornet Bay

Camp leaders pose at the flagpole in the mid-1930s. Most of these leaders came from the National Park Service and United States Forest Service.

Cornet Bay

Above:
Al Davis, Camp Foreman, stands on the left, and other camp leaders sit and stand with him in front of the flagpole, 1934.

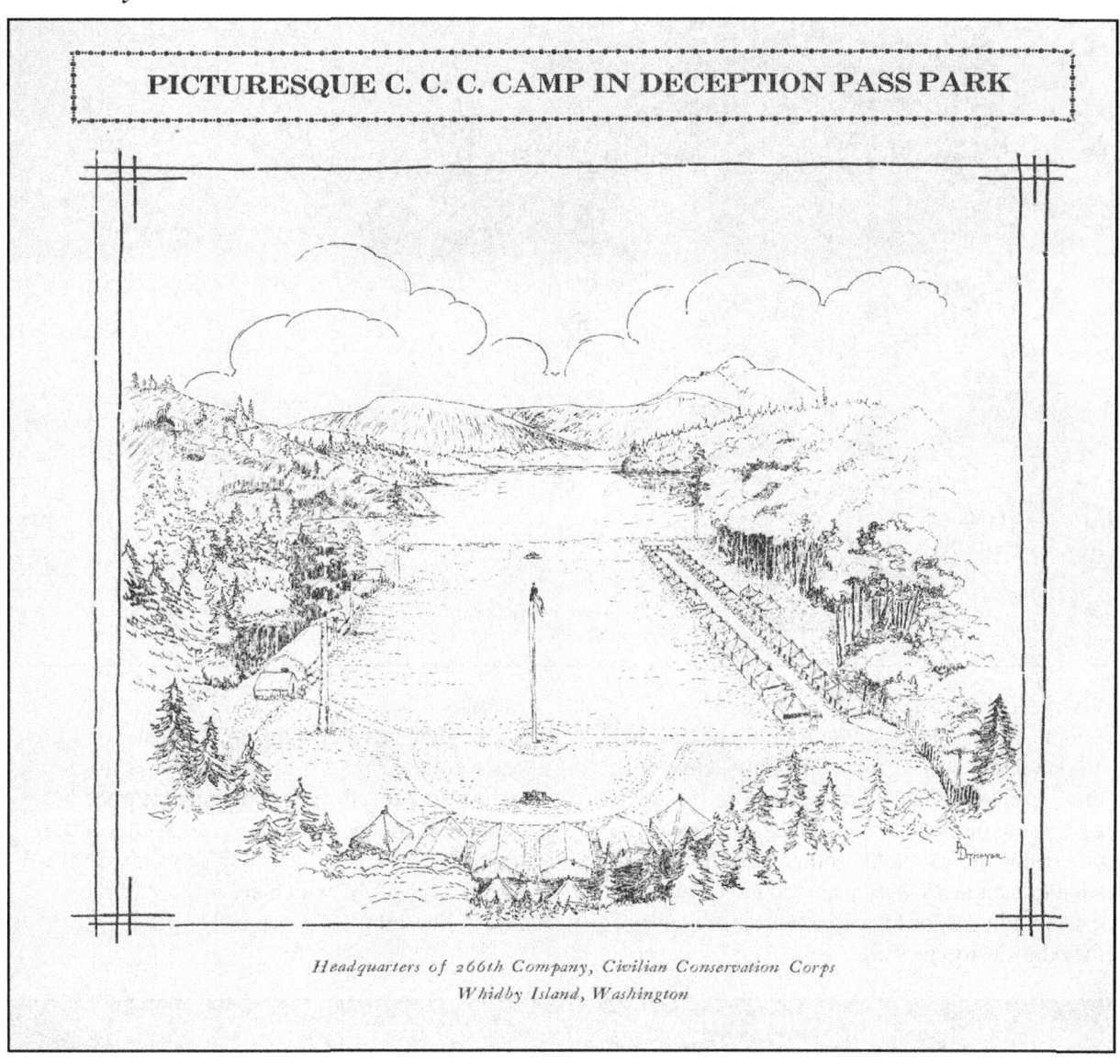

Cornet Bay

PICTURESQUE C. C. C. CAMP IN DECEPTION PASS PARK

Headquarters of 266th Company, Civilian Conservation Corps
Whidby Island, Washington

Above:
A hand-drawn sketch of the camp, looking towards the northeast.

Cornet Bay

Above:
The beginning stages of the rock fireplace and amphitheater at the camp. There are actually three fireplaces: the main fireplace on the right side of the picture, and one on each wing wall, one visible here near the center of the photo. The smaller fireplaces were intended to be used for warming ovens, or to keep people sitting near the edges warm as well.

Below:
Making the hearth for the amphitheater and fireplace at the camp. Using granite rocks from nearby sources, the crew members learned how to cut rock, shape it, build a wall and mortar it properly. This fireplace sits fairly close to the waters of the bay, which are just out of the picture to the right.

Cornet Bay

Above:
The fireplace is completed, and now awaits the development of the seating for the amphitheater.

Photograph from the Washington State Digital Archives.

Below:
Camp as seen from Cornet Bay, looking south.
Photo courtesy of John Tursi.

Cornet Bay

Above:
Service trucks line up parked under a shed. Various maintenance buildings now stand on the grounds, with some of the local expert men standing in front. View looking south, towards where the current entrance road joins the parking lot, and about where the current maintenance sheds are now located.

Below:
The new tool shed stood outside the main gate of the camp, in this view looking towards the northeast. When the Cornet Bay CCC camp ended in the new decade, nearly all of these buildings were removed. Today, the outline of the camp is reflected in the retreat center layout, almost matching the CCC design.

EAST CRANBERRY LAKE

When Deception Pass first became a state park, the eastern shores of Cranberry Lake were already popular with local communities as a gathering place for swimming, picnicking, and neighborhood potlucks.

With the beaches vacated by the military, allowing the general public to enjoy the saltwater shoreline here for the first time, the popularity of Cranberry Lake did not wane.

The National Park Service recognized the value of this freshwater lake for recreation. They designed their master plan to focus on the access to the saltwater beaches while maintaining and improving the opportunities to enjoy the lakeshore as well.

Some simple buildings had already been constructed along the lakeshore when the area became a park to accommodate the many people recreating in this area.

The Civilian Conservation Corps replaced these buildings with several new facilities, built in the classic rustic style. These facilities included a large picnic shelter not far from the shore, a large bathhouse and concession stand directly above the beach and dock, a restroom behind the bathhouse and another one further south, and two small picnic shelters, one to each side of the swimming beach.

Other facilities included improvements to the swim beach with a rock wall and walkways, an improved parking lot, and a pump house.

At the time of the CCC, the park entrance was a quarter mile to the north of this area. East Cranberry Lake relaxed at the end of the road, but as a popular swimming hole, it was the focus of most of the day use activity.

With the later development of West Beach in the 1950s, the popularity of East Cranberry faded, leaving a quiet lakeshore enjoyed by fishermen, wedding planners, and other special events.

Today the new park entrance comes in right next to the lakeshore, giving first-time visitors a chance to see what was at that time the busiest and most popular part of the park.

This quiet picnic and fishing area is now a relaxing haven away from the busier areas of the park.

This chapter will look at the photographic record of the development of all of these additions, starting with the lakeshore buildings, then the large shelter.

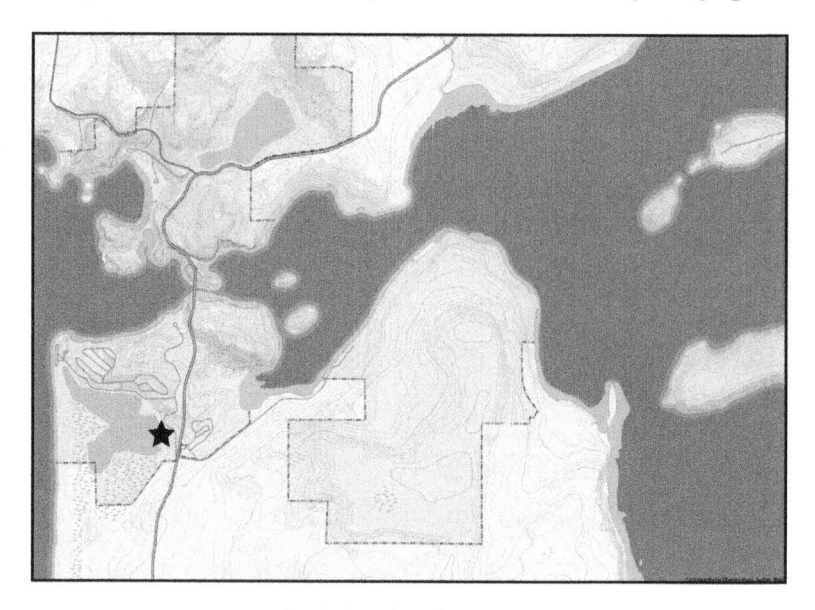

East Cranberry Lake

Above:
CCC members plant trees along the south border of the park near Cranberry Lake, to screen the park land from nearby neighbors. Park shelters and restroom facilities are being built in the woods behind them.

Below:
Horses draw grading plows after cutting the forests down to open up the East Cranberry area for recreation. Firewood is stacked in the background for use back at the camp at Cornet Bay. Smoke rises behind the enrollees from a slash pile burn.

East Cranberry Lake

Above:
Starting the masonry wall along the shores of Cranberry Lake. This wall will become the edge of the swimming beach, which for many years was perhaps the most popular attraction at Deception Pass.

Below:
The seawall continues to grow. The two sheds are apparently bath houses that pre-date the CCC. The words on the side and back of the near shed say "Ladies Bath House." Presumably the other building was the men's.

East Cranberry Lake

Above:
The seawall is now nearly complete, defining the edge of the swim beach. The rock wall can still be found today, but the swim beach has been neglected for so long, passed over for the new beach at the other end of the lake.

Below:
The structures from before the CCC era are removed. Although they served their purpose, these buildings were not created to harmonize with the environment or to create an architecturally consistent landscape.

East Cranberry Lake

Above:
One of the first buildings to be completed at the east end of Cranberry Lake is the pump house. This building is still in place today, although not in use, and in an out of the way location near the park boundary, so it is seldom seen by park visitors.

It is one of the park's more poorly constructed examples of CCC work, perhaps because it is one of the first. It uses mixed stone types and less detailed mortaring than is seen throughout the park in future work.

View looking northwest.

Above:
One of the environmental hazards of life on Whidbey Island is windstorms. A windstorm in November of 1934 dropped two large grand fir trees onto the recently built pump house .

View looking southwest.

Photograph from the Washington State Digital Archives.

East Cranberry Lake

Above and below:
At the north end of the East Cranberry Lake development, CCC workers built a small but very distinctive picnic shelter. It has room for a small stove and one picnic table. The roofline with its extension on one side is distinctive.
Photographs from the Washington State Digital Archives.

East Cranberry Lake

Above:
The same shelter, looking northeast from near the lakeshore. This look was modified and simplified in the seventies, then re-built in 2011 to once again look like this original design.

Photograph from the Washington State Digital Archives.

East Cranberry Lake

Above:
One of the first buildings to be built at East Cranberry was what they called in their Army vernacular "the latrine." We know it as the East Cranberry restroom, a modest but appropriately sized facility for the area.

Extra efforts were made to keep the foundation rocks from forming lines, trying to achieve a randomness of size and shapes.

Below:
The intricacies of fitting the logs together tightly can be seen, as another log is prepared for fitting at the top. This was time consuming work that gives us buildings that are still tight fitting today.

East Cranberry Lake

Above:
The rockwork on the restroom done now, the logs are going up one at
a time, and the interior work begins. It appears that the CCC built a roof over the building to shelter the workers. You can see this shelter in the next photograph as well.

Below:
Now the shakes go on, row by row, course by course. Back then, the cedar trees available for making shakes were big enough to create shakes that were 36 inches long. Today it is expensive to find trees big enough to replace shakes with this authentic size.

East Cranberry Lake

Above:
With the roof nearly done, Corps members stand in front of the restroom, proud of their work.

Below:
Enrollees mix the concrete for the floors of the latrine.

East Cranberry Lake

Above:
The finished product, the restroom at East Cranberry. The original hand-wrought door hardware is still in use. However, the ridgepole at the top that overhangs the roof no longer exists, and the honey color of the wood has been stained a chocolate brown, as have nearly all of the CCC buildings, unfortunately. View looking northwest. Cranberry Lake can be seen in the background.

East Cranberry Lake

Above:
Built just a stone's throw from the water's edge, the bathhouse at East Cranberry was expected to be the center of lakeshore activity, containing a concession store and changing rooms. The rockwork done, the logs are now being fitted for the roof. View looking south. The changing room built before the CCC is visible on the right side of the picture near the lakeshore.

Below:
The bathhouse is nearly done now, with shakes being placed on the roof. In the background behind the bathhouse, the rock fireplace exterior of the kitchen shelter can be seen, along with the lake to the left.

View looking north toward kitchen shelter beyond.

East Cranberry Lake

East Cranberry Lake

Previous page:
The bathhouse at East Cranberry, as seen from the north looking toward the south and southwest. The sign near the middle on the tree says "Restrooms" with an arrow pointing left beyond the bathhouse, to the restroom seen in previous pages.

Above:
The left hand side of the bathhouse, or the north side, looking east. The roofed portion on the left covers the actual changing room. The open space behind the log wall on the near side of the roof is the common area leading to the several changing rooms. This pattern was repeated on the right side for the women.
Between the two changing rooms is a concession store, here barely visible beneath the roof on the right.

Page 4 shows an architectural drawing of this building as seen from above.

East Cranberry Lake

Above:
A closer view of the bathhouse, with a customer at the concession window.

Albert H. Good notes the simple, practical plan combining a minor food concession without interfering with the bathhouse function. He goes on to say "the disposition, unfortunately general, to litter concessions with advertising signs is here evidenced. Behind the signs there will be found a very attractive building."

Note the box hanging upside down on the side of the tree on the left, with the words "Dish Soap."

East Cranberry Lake

Above:
The bathhouse shelter in use, shortly after it opened. It was used as a concession building in the middle section, and as changing rooms with men on the left and women on the right.

Photo taken from near the lakeshore, looking east.

In 1970, a contract was awarded to a local company to remove the foundation of this building and level the ground where it stood. What happened, and why, between 1935 when it was completed and 1970 just thirty-five years later when the last vestiges were removed is unknown.

East Cranberry Lake

Above:
The next building to be constructed at East Cranberry Lake is the large kitchen shelter near the lakeshore. Masonry workers establish the base of the picnic shelter in the photo above. This appears to be the southwest corner.

Below:
Masonry work continues on the shelter as the foundation is established. Local experienced men (LEMs) taught the enrollees how to do quality work, thus building future employable skills for Corps members while accomplishing the immediate tasks of building a park.

East Cranberry Lake

Above:
The logs for the shelter are first laid out for fitting, in preparation for installation on top of the rock foundation. Cranberry Lake can be seen in the background.

Below:
With the foundation complete, the logs can now be laid on top of the rocks. The shelter starts to take shape. South wall, looking north.

East Cranberry Lake

Above:
Southwest corner, looking northeast.

Below:
With the log framing of the walls complete, the rafters can now be placed for the roof.

Each shelter at Deception Pass built with logs atop a rock foundation uses the rocks in a unique way. Other distinctive features unique to individual shelters include shingle-covered walls and lap siding.

East Cranberry Lake

Left:
The fireplace is built into the interior of the north wall of the shelter.

Below:
The stoves on the south side of the shelter are framed in, sharing a common chimney out the south side. Firebrick inside the firebox is intended to keep the mortar of the rockwork from weakening and loosening over time. The triple firebox design sharing a common chimney is unusual.

East Cranberry Lake

Above:
Shakes are now nearly finished being installed on the roof of the shelter. Landscaping has not yet begun. View looking west toward the lake.

Below:
With the roof in place, the floor can now be poured as the crew mixes concrete and pours it out by the wheelbarrow load.

East Cranberry Lake

Top:
Workers finish the chimney of the fireplace, in the cold weather of January, 1935. The windows have yet to be installed.

Right:
The top of the chimney, expanded to show the men doing the work on the chimney.

East Cranberry Lake

Above:
Crew members kneel at the back side of the completed shelter. The shelter is distinctive from all the other shelters in the park with the dual chimneys, one at each end, the horizontal logs separated by three columns of rock on each side, and the shingle eaves above the logs.

Below:
The south wall of the shelter, showing the three-stove system ready to be used by visitors. This picture is taken from about the middle of the shelter.

East Cranberry Lake

Above:
The East Cranberry Lake shelter, ready for use in 1935. The design of this building for CCC development is unique to the Washington State Park system, representing a park ranger's scheme to achieve a look that is "pleasantly different."

Below:
The north wall, with two pieces of furniture made onsite by creative crew members.

East Cranberry Lake

Above:
The lakeshore south of the kitchen shelter, looking south. The bathhouse is barely in view at the left, the dock out of view to the right. Note the CCC-created wooden benches.

The sign just left of center on the tree in the distance says, "Leave No _____ On Grounds" (illegible word has five letters). Left of that sign is a box attached to a tree. The box says, "Rinso." The benches are thoroughly covered with graffiti carved into them. Photograph from the Washington State Digital Archives.

Below:
The northeast side of the large East Cranberry shelter, looking southwest.

East Cranberry Lake

Above:
Cranberry Lake on a sunny afternoon. It appears this picture was taken before the CCC did their work, as the building on the left is the old changing room that the CCC removed. Eventually, a boardwalk would encircle the swimming area between the shore and the diving board in the lake. The photographer captured someone diving into the water from the left hand diving board.

Photograph from the Washington State Digital Archives.

Below:
The upper lot of the East Cranberry Lake parking lot on a rather busy day, filled with modern cars of that era. The bathhouse and restroom are to the left; the picnic shelter is just out of the picture in the background and a little to the left.

59

East Cranberry Lake

Above:
East Cranberry as seen from the diving tower in the lake. Bathhouse is in the upper left. The dock can now be seen, forming a promenade around the swimming area.

Photograph from the Washington State Digital Archives.

East Cranberry Lake

Above:
One of the CCC buildings rises above the crowd on the left at the East Cranberry Lake parking area. The occasion of this gathering is unknown.

Below:
The park has always been popular, even from the very beginning. The *Farm Bureau News* hosted annual summertime picnics at Cranberry Lake to have politicians and business people talk about building a bridge across the pass; this may have been one of those gatherings.

Photograph from the Washington State Digital Archives.

East Cranberry Lake

Above:
Cars line up on the new highway, which has become a parking lot for Oak Harbor residents attending the annual picnic at Cranberry Lake. The parking area inside the gates holds well over 150 cars; it looks like at least that many outside the gate as well.

View looking south from near the old entrance. At the bottom of the hill is the current Cornet Bay Road intersection and a traffic light. In 1935, it was just trees.

Photograph from the Washington State Digital Archives.

OLD ENTRANCE

"Old entrance" would have meant nothing to the CCC camp workers. The park entrance was the park entrance. It had been in use for at least twenty years or more by the time the CCC camps worked at the park.

The CCC built a caretaker house next to the entrance so that the ranger could greet visitors as they came into the park and monitor traffic throughout the day and night. And in turn, visitors could see where the ranger lived in case they wanted to stop by and chat, share a cup of coffee, or inform the caretaker of a problem in the park.

Over the years, because of the increase in traffic into and out of the park onto a high-speed highway, at a bend in the roadway, there were just far too many conflicts caused by the design of the entrance. Turning into the park from the south meant blocking traffic until there was a gap in the line of cars coming from the opposite direction. And leaving the park meant waiting for a gap in traffic from both directions while also negotiating around the turning vehicles trying to get into the park that were also creating their own bottleneck.

Accidents and near misses were common. Frustrations and anxiety were abundant. And the park ranger and his family could not live in a fishbowl with millions of visitors driving by the front door, or stopping to get directions, pay their campsite fee, or have that cup of coffee.

It was perfectly clear that this park entrance was not going to work any longer.

In the nineties, Washington State Parks and Washington Department of Transportation officials planned out a new entrance to the south, just north of where Cornet Bay Road entered the highway. They re-designed Cornet Bay Road to meet the highway at a right angle, and planned a new entrance to the park at this intersection. With a traffic signal to smooth out the conflicts, the new entrance opened in 1997.

The entrance lane into the park still backed up traffic onto the highway, however, because it was only a single lane, with the park registration booth inside just a hundred meters or so.

In 2004, a second lane was added to the new entrance, giving space for vehicles to queue up as they waited to register, and relieving further pressure from the highway intersection.

The old entrance? It was gated, and became a historical asterisk. This made for a much quieter residence for the occupants of the caretaker's house built here by the CCC.

The house is still occupied by park staff today. The CCC-built garage nearby is now reserved for park equipment storage instead of the resident's personal use.

This chapter looks at the construction of the house and garage, located next to what we now call the "old entrance."

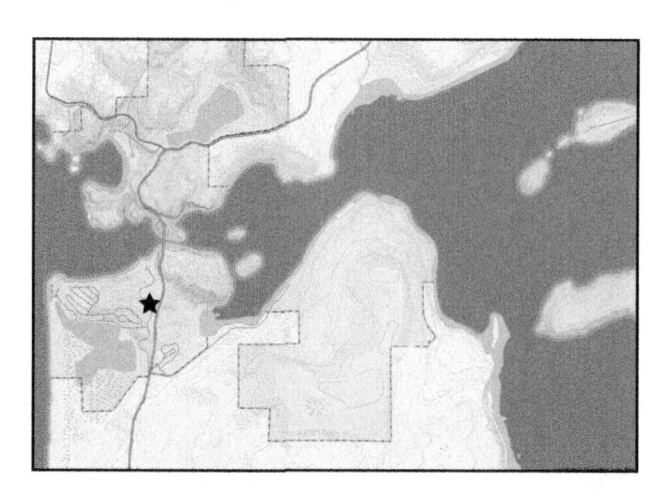

Old Entrance

Old Entrance

Previous page:
The original Whidbey Island entrance of the park looking north up the new highway.

The sign points left for Cranberry Lake, Cornet Bay, and North Beach. Access to Cornet Bay was via the new underpass. The sign points to the right, or south, for Oak Harbor, Coupeville, and Columbia Beach, where the Mukilteo ferry now docks on Whidbey.

Above:
Logs have been peeled, and are now being hewed for making log purlins of the new caretaker's house to be built between Cranberry Lake and the park entrance.

Below:
Granite stones are being cut and shaped for the foundation of the new caretaker's house.

Old Entrance

Above:
Peeling logs for the new caretaker's cabin near the park entrance on Highway 20, south of the bridge.

Below:
Mixing concrete to pour the foundation of the caretaker's residence.

Old Entrance

Above:
The forms are prepared for the pouring of the foundation for the cabin.

Below:
Pouring fresh concrete into the foundation forms.

Old Entrance

Above:
Joists were laid across the foundation walls, tied into the first row of logs to form the base of the house. View looking basically west from the east side of the house.

Below:
Log number three of the caretaker's house, as the walls start to go up. Nearly everything was done by hand, so moving logs took great care and ingenuity, along with precise measurements and cutting.

Old Entrance

Above:
Most of the logs are up for the base walls, ready to climb to the peak walls. A stock of logs wait at the base for building the roof.

Below:
The foundation of the garage for the caretaker's house gets ready for pouring. The garage is just south of the house.

Old Entrance

Above:
The first and second course of logs go on the foundation of the garage. Meanwhile, work continues on the house itself, and the walls rise to the eventual peak of the roof.

View looking north.

Right:
Building the firebox of the fireplace. Compare this with the finished picture on page 75.

Old Entrance

Above:
Difficult work gets complex as well, joining the walls to a new roof line. The main beams and purlins are being pulled into place.

Below:
And a roof log goes onto the garage as well. Look at the number of men on the right required to hold up the log, using 2x4s to hold it high above their heads, while others on the left hold the log down at that end.

"We made all the hardware in the fireplaces in the kitchens, all of that was done by us. It was an opportunity, if you were willing. You could learn a lot that helped you later in life. I followed that trade throughout my life."

—John Tursi

Old Entrance

Above:
With the roof framed in, work can now begin on the finishing touches of the fireplace. View from the north, looking southeast. The garage is behind the house, the entrance road behind the photographer.

Below:
The roof line is nearly done on the garage now, as seen from the side porch of the caretaker's house.

Old Entrance

Above:
The house and garage are basically done, with just the detail and landscaping work left to do.

View looking eastward.

Below:
Skilled worker cutting roof purlins with precision.

Old Entrance

Above:
The interior of the caretaker's cabin, set up for a ceremonial dinner in the living room. Other than the furnishings, the appearance of this room has hardly changed at all in eighty years.

Below:
The western side of the house, looking east toward the new highway, just out of site below the crest of the ground. The garage sits off to the right. The deer in the foreground must be munching on new landscaping.

Old Entrance

Old Entrance

Previous Page:
Two views of the caretaker's cabin.

Both photographs from the Washington State Digital Archives.

Above:
Caretaker's garage, seen from the caretaker's side yard. View looking southeast.

Photograph from the Washington State Digital Archives.

NORTH BEACH

It was supposed to be the main attraction for all of Deception Pass State Park. National Park planners designed the entrance road to come down to North Beach so that visitors could drive through old growth forests, get close to the beach in their vehicles, and after a short hike take in the sights of the waters of Deception Pass and the bridge above.

A side road was added with an underpass beneath Highway 20 to get to Cornet Bay. A visitor center was planned for the North Beach area to interpret the magnificent forests and marine environment all around.

But this area never became the focus of the park. Maybe the road was too steep, or the beach too rocky or the currents too swift. The center was never built, and the underpass below Highway 20 became a trail instead of a roadway.

It may not have achieved popularity, but those who know the park know that North Beach is a delightful place to stroll with friends, a family, a loved one, or all alone. The nearly mile long shoreline stretches in a photogenic sweeping curve out to West Point, with driftwood lining the beach and tall firs pointing heavenward above.

The CCC built three shelters along the waterfront for those visitors who now come looking for beauty, for peace and quiet, for a challenging hike along the pass, or for salmon to catch from the beach in odd-numbered years.

They also built a typical CCC restroom, and the associated water lines, sewer systems, and other infrastructure still in use today.

And to connect to the bridge above, the Corps members engineered a trail that contours down the steep slopes from the bridge level down to sea level, a drop of over 50 meters in less than 400 meters. Rock walls line the trail to reduce erosion onto the trail from the hillsides above.

The scenery here is breathtaking. The facilities constructed by the CCC complement these magnificent surroundings.

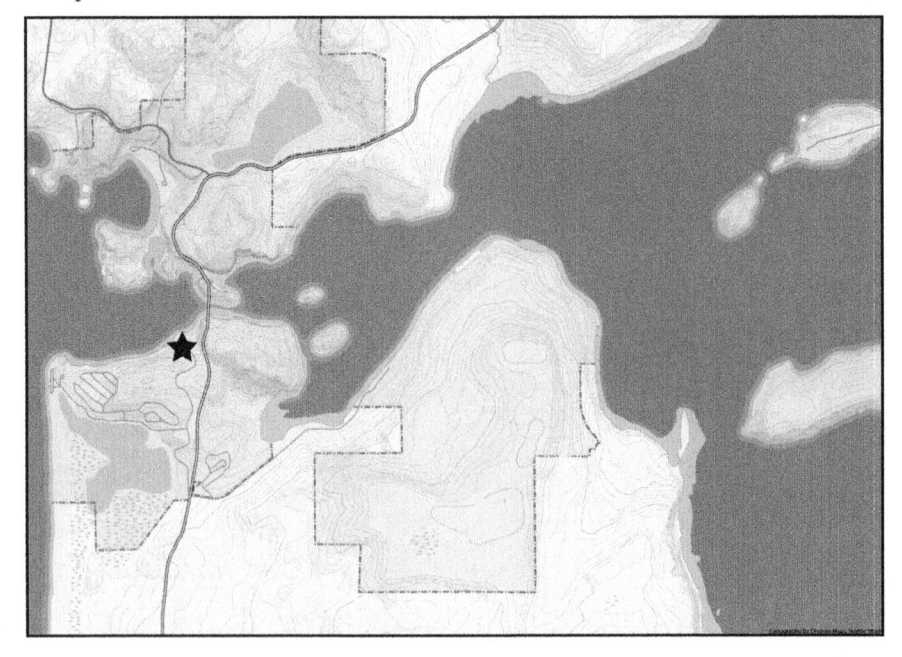

North Beach

Above:
It may be a bit unorthodox, but enrollees are here at North Beach landing lumber at the beach to be used for building shelters nearby. Considering the currents of the pass that can run at speeds of up to eight knots through here, it appears they chose to pole and paddle the raft through the pass at slack tide.

Below:
The shelter under construction at Little North Beach, the small beach almost directly under the bridge. The trail up to the restroom can be seen climbing the hill in the back. This shelter has been accused of not being authentic CCC construction. It is true that the quality is less than the other buildings, but from these pictures, it appears it may have been the first one built by the Corps members, and thus a learning opportunity.

North Beach

Left:
Detail of the northwest column, and a closer view of the water pump located just outside the shelter.

Right:
Looking inside the shelter at the stove. This shelter has a short sidewall around three of the sides.

North Beach

Above:
The Little North Beach shelter shown from the east side. The waters of Deception Pass are to the right about a hundred meters. The bridge is behind the photographer about four hundred meters, and about fifty meters higher.

Below:
Albert Good had a rather caustic comment about this shelter. "Realization that the superlative timber resources of this area have not been conducive to the development of a sound masonry technique," he wrote, "tempers somewhat a critical sputtering of the unorthodox masonry here pictured."

North Beach

Above:
The large shelter at North Beach is west of the Little North Beach area, just west of Gun Point. Here, the shelter framing is going up on the roof. The four posts and the four main beams are up, and now the roof line is being established.

Below:
The rafters have been built onto the roof beams and ridge line, and now the purlins, the horizontal structural pieces, are being attached.

North Beach

Above:
The finished shelter at North Beach, with the sand of the beach leading right to the entrance. This shelter also has the low walls skirting the building, with all four sides walled in.

Below:
Nine of the enrollees pose in front of the shelter at North Beach, justifiably proud of their work. No rocks were used for this building other than for the stove, as the building is all post and beam.

Photo courtesy of John Tursi.

North Beach

Above:
The only National Park Service picture of the North Beach restroom, shown here looking westward at the east side of the building. The entrance to the men's side of the restroom is on the near side. North Beach is down the trail to the right.

This restroom is above the beach, adjacent to the parking area.

North Beach

Two views of North Beach.

Above:
Taken near where the kitchen shelter would be built, also shows a foundation for the bridge under construction on Pass Island in the upper left of the photo.

Right:
Photographed later after the bridge was completed, taken from the headland west of Gun Point, west of where the kitchen shelters were built.

BUILDING THE HIGHWAY
WHIDBEY ISLAND SIDE

With funding for the bridge secured by federal WPA grants and the state legislature, the two CCC camps were asked to build the highway approaches to the new bridge.

Camp Deception Pass on the Whidbey side built over a kilometer of roadway leading up from the low ground near Cranberry Lake almost at sea level to the edge of the pass, 55 meters above the water.

Most of the terrain was relatively straightforward until they got near the pass, where a large shoulder of Goose Rock lay in their path. This they blasted through with dynamite, creating the gap in the rock that we drive through today just south of the bridge.

The new highway also had to bisect the new park road between Cornet Bay and North Beach. Rather than have a dangerous intersection along the highway to interrupt traffic, the CCC would build an underpass for the park road.

If you want to win a bet, show a group of local people a picture of the Highway 20 underpass, and ask if anyone in the group knows where the underpass can be found in the park.

Then to really get them flustered, share that they have probably driven over this underpass a hundred times if not a thousand times.

The highway underpass is a marvelous piece of engineering and construction, yet it remains one of the most unrecognized and unknown features of Deception Pass State Park. And it is there hiding in plain site.

The following pictures capture some of the work of the CCC crews in building the highway approach to the future bridge and the underpass nearby, from removing the trees and bedrock to smoothing out the soon-to-be-used roadbed.

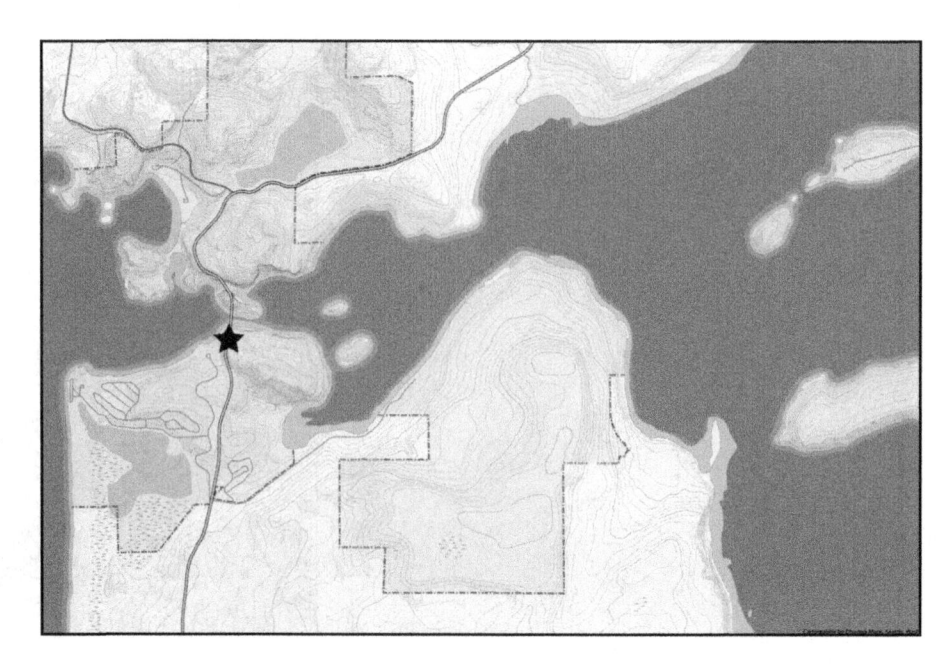

Highway 20, Whidbey Side

Highway 20, Whidbey Side

Previous page:
The view from the north tip of Whidbey Island across Deception Pass to Pass Island, before the bridge. Beyond Pass Island and out of sight is Canoe Pass. Fidalgo Island rises beyond that.

Right:
The CCC workers only had cross cut saws and axes available to remove the trees along the route of the new highway. On the rightt, the man in the middle holds a crosscut saw, while his companions hold axes next to what appears to be the last large tree standing.

Below:
Two enrollees using a crosscut saw to cut down a very large tree on a very steep slope near the pass. The man on the right stands on a springboard, a platform notched into the tree for a place to stand, allowing him to cut above the tougher wood near the roots.

Highway 20, Whidbey Side

Standing on the edge of the cliff overlooking the pass, three workers take on the last remaining trees.

Left:
Two workers hold a crosscut saw, creating the falling cut, having already cut the backside with a notch cut.

Right:
They finish the falling cut or backcut, and stand to watch as the tree falls down toward the pass. (Hard hats and other safety gear and safe felling methods were not commonly used yet.)

Pass Island is just across the water in the background, and the steep cliffs of Bowman Hill rise above Pass Island. Pass Island may have been burned from time to time by local tribal peoples to encourage the growth of camas, preventing trees from establishing a large forest on the island.

Highway 20, Whidbey Side

Probably more than any other forestry tool, the crosscut saw requires precision teamwork as much as strength. Two men working as a team can almost make a crosscut saw sing.

You can see the pride in these workers as they hold the crosscut saw in poses near the location of the new bridge connection.

90

Highway 20, Whidbey Side

Above:
The slopes of the road are cleaned and shaped for the new highway, which is just now beginning to take shape.

Below:
The highway has been roughed in. The man on the far left holds a pickaxe, while the men on the right hold shovels and rakes as they smooth out the road cut leading toward the bridge. View appears to be looking north towards the old park entrance.

Highway 20, Whidbey Side

Above:
Sometimes it is easier to blast out a large stump than dig it up by hand. The slope is nearly completed here. Pieces of debris shoot across the road in this dramatic photo.

Below:
The blasting crew members pose for a picture in between blasting as they remove the rock for the highway route at the bridge. The rock behind them is part of Goose Rock. The bridge will connect with Whidbey Island near here.

Photo courtesy of John Tursi.

Highway 20, Whidbey Side

Above:
The men set charges.

Below:
The blast is triggered, removing a large amount of debris, with blast material visible to the right of the blast cloud.

Both photos courtesy of John Tursi.

Highway 20, Whidbey Side

Two views of the rock cut just south of the bridge.

Above:
A steam shovel helps remove debris as men on the hillside plan where more charges will be placed. View looking north about one hundred meters from the bridge.

Right:
Trucks dump the debris blasted out of the rock down the steep embankment to build up the edge of the new highway.

View looking south from the top of the rock west of the highway, south of the bridge, toward the bend in the road that heads southeast toward the underpass.

Highway 20, Whidbey Side

Above:
A steam shovel helps move rock just south of the bridge. Here the workers had to cut through about one hundred meters of rock to create a level approach to the bridge, which has its cliff-side apron
already completed in this picture. Trucks and even a trailer pulled by a car haul the debris away to finish the roadbed.

The parking lot south of the bridge is already taking shape, visible on the left side of the photo. On the right, the shoulder of Goose Rock comes down to meet a temporary work building.

Photo taken from the rock hillside west of the bridge, south of the present day parking lot. Pass Island is in the background, and the waters of the pass can bee seen in the upper right side of the photo.

Highway 20, Whidbey Side

Above:
View from North Beach as the foundations for the bridge on Pass Island take shape. The Canoe Pass span is already underway. The long exposure of the camera smooth out the water of the pass into a marble-like consistency.

Below:
Now the main span reaches out from Pass Island toward Whidbey Island.

Highway 20, Whidbey Side

Looking from the new span on Pass Island toward the Whidbey Island side where the arching bottom of the bridge structure is now in place. The water is just out of the camera's view below the main bridge abutment at the bottom of the picture.

Highway 20, Whidbey Side

Above:
On July 31, 1935, people from both sides of the bridge gather to celebrate the opening of the Deception Pass Bridge, or technically, bridges. The main span is hidden by the abundance of people enjoying the new connection. The men of the CCC who built the highway approaches to the bridge are most likely out on the bridge enjoying the celebration, and the view.

Highway 20, Whidbey Side

Above:
One challenging addition to building the highway approach from the south side was adding an underpass about four hundred meters south of the bridge. Most drivers today do not even know this exists, yet thousands of cars drive over it every day.

The park road system planned by the National Park Service required a roadway to join North Beach with Cornet Bay. The new highway would bisect this roadway, so an underpass had to be built. The next few pictures highlight some of the many steps required to build this underpass.

Above, workers had to first build log cribs as the initial framework for the underpass. Notice the size of the logs, put into place with nothing but block and tackle.

Highway 20, Whidbey Side

Both of these pictures were taken from the side of Goose Rock, looking towards the southwest.

Above:
The framework for the foundation can be seen rising in the cut.

Below:
The foundation secure, the lattice work begins to rise, to eventually allow the highway to be built overhead.

Highway 20, Whidbey Side

Above:
Almost to grade level with the highway now, the photo shows the way that the CCC worked: by hand with hand tools for the most part. View looking southeast from the bed of the future highway.

Below:
A narrow plank connects the highway bed with the platform of the new bridge for the underpass. In this view towards the northwest, Goose Rock rises steeply on the right; the deep channels of the pass are around the corner up ahead.

Highway 20, Whidbey Side

Left:
John Tursi, holding the saw, and other CCC workers prepare materials for the underpass construction.

Both photos courtesy of John Tursi.

Below:
John Tursi driving a large truck to bring materials to the worksite. U.S.D.I. stands for the United States Department of the Interior, which includes the National Park Service, one of the four leading partners in the management of the Civilian Conservation Corps.

Highway 20, Whidbey Side

Above:
Looking southward again, the bridge base has been built. Reinforcement bar (re-bar) has been placed in preparation for the concrete to be poured in this frame.

Below:
The first part of the highway has now been poured. The railing is also in place, forms for the railing holding the freshly poured concrete inside. The railing is still visible today.

Highway 20, Whidbey Side

Above:
While the highway base is built, other workers are now finishing the underpass portion. The walls are being covered by the typical rockwork found throughout the park structures.

Below:
With scaffolding in place, the workers can now reach the entire wall of the underpass and bring the rock siding to the top.

Highway 20, Whidbey Side

Above:
This view shows the completed tunnel, and the rockwork progressing on the face of the underpass/bridge.

Below:
Now the rockwork is done. The detail work in the rock face shows larger rocks at the base, smaller rocks at the top, with care taken not to have rows or columns. If this is the same view as the previous picture, and from the trees in the background it likely is, then it appears that the rockwork has changed next to the tunnel since the above picture was taken.

CAMP ROSARIO BEACH

While enrollees at Cornet Bay were primarily from the East Coast, the 948th Company at Rosario Beach was made up of men from Washington and Oregon. The two groups were kept separate because of perceived cultural differences.

Planned as a tandem camp with the Cornet Bay side, the Rosario camp's mission was to develop facilities on the north side of the Pass. Without a bridge, the two camps were close in proximity but worked on separate projects with somewhat different guidelines and building methods.

In November of 1933, the first campers arrived, and built a camp between Rosario Beach and an area called Cougar Gap on southwest Fidalgo Island. Built on the side of a steep rock hill, the camp area lacked the flat parade field grounds of Cornet Bay, making camp life an uphill or downhill issue with every building and roadway.

Enrollees spent the first six months of the camp reducing fire hazard debris, building trails, and building roads from Pass Lake to Reservation Bay, almost all of which was done entirely with hand tools and wheelbarrows.

The second six months brought more trail building, and gathering materials for the Reservation Bay caretaker's house, two kitchens, and a latrine. Granite came from all parts of the park. Logs came from Hoypus Hill, boomed and brought through the pass by boat.

The third camp enrollees had the privilege of building the water system and power line from Rosario Beach to Reservation Bay, and constructing the caretaker's house. Remnants of the water line system can still be found in the well house at Rosario and a storage tank high on the bluff between Rosario and Bowman Bay.

This camp also took on the task of building the roadway approach to the north side of the soon-to-be-built Deception Pass Bridge. Of the two camps, Rosario Camp had the harder highway challenge, having to negotiate the shoreline of Pass Lake and the severe rock slopes north of the bridge.

Hardly a trace of the camp can be found at this time. It sat on private property that was leased for the duration of the camp. Since then, new homes have been developed over some of the camp area. However, the work that the campers accomplished in the park will continue as their legacy long into the future.

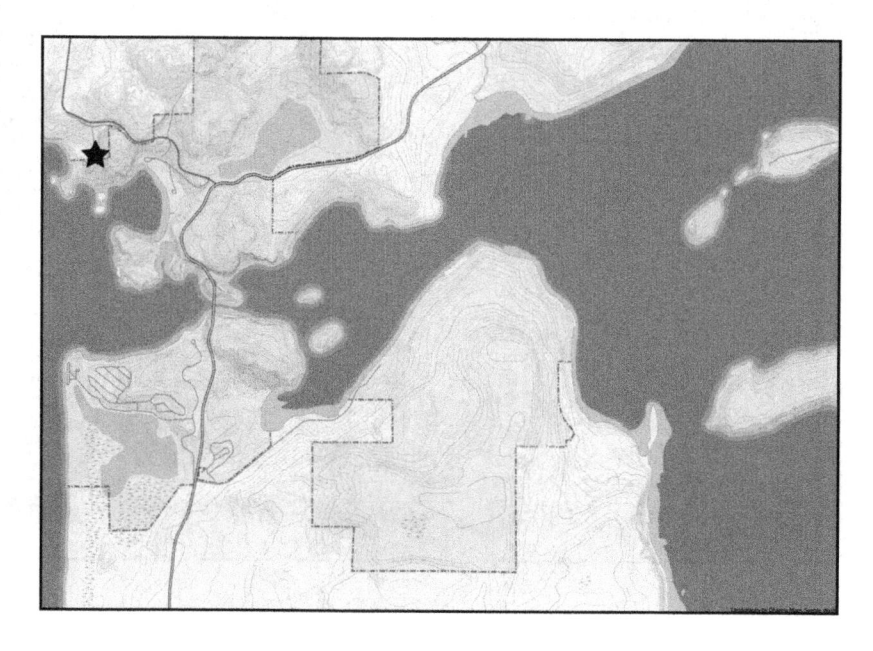

Camp Rosario Beach

Set on the sloping hill above Rosario Beach, Camp Rosario had terrain issues to overcome. The shape and slopes limited the ability to have a parade field like Cornet Bay. The advantage was a slightly drier site that certainly drained well.

In this view, from the higher ridge of Cougar Gap above the camp, the camp can be seen tucked up tightly to the talus slope of Rosario Hill on the left. The barracks are on the left, the cookhouse in the shadows towards the water, and various administrative buildings to the right and in the foreground. Rosario Bay is beyond the trees in the center, about 400 meters beyond.

Camp Rosario Beach

Above:
These buildings were personnel quarters for officers and leaders. View looking northwest.

Below:
The flagpole is planted near the middle of what was called Company Street.

View looking westward.

Camp Rosario Beach

Above:
Rows of barracks point toward the water, with the talus slope of the hill to the left. The flagpole area is seen to the far right.

View looking southwestward.

Below:
Inside the barracks. Since the camps were run under military discipline, the enrollees took great care to leave the barracks in precise cleanliness and order.

Camp Rosario Beach

Above:
Inside the mess hall, rows upon rows of table settings wait for the crew members to come to their meal. The cooks and servers pose in the background. View looking southerly, with the afternoon sun coming in the open windows on the right.

"I volunteered for table waiter. Finally the cook started working with me, and I started helping him. And the first thing you know I was assistant cook ... Whenever you want pancakes for three hundred people, I know the recipe."

—Ralph Brown, enrollee

110

Camp Rosario Beach

The same mess hall, as seen from where the cooks were standing. On the back wall are two crossed pick axes on the left, two crossed shovels on the right, and a banner between them that says, as best we can read:

Winners
The State Park
Field Day
[unreadable]
Deception
CCC Camp
Presented by
Anacortes
Chamber
Of Commerce

Camp Rosario Beach

Administrative buildings for Camp Rosario Beach, tucked up close to the talus slopes of the hill that separates Rosario from Reservation Bay. The building on the left is the superintendent's office. In the middle is a motor pool building with five bays. On the right is a tool sharpening shed.

Camp Rosario Beach

Both of these photos are labeled "work crew at noon."

It is hard to tell where either of these photos were taken, both being on a beach somewhere. Both are of Rosario enrollees is all we can say for certain.

The photo above has a sign pointing left that says "Deception Pass" and two unreadable words underneath.

The photo below has men in rain slickers and hats, but no other identifying marks.

113

Camp Rosario Beach

Above:
Labeled "work crew", this photo shows a mixture of ages and clothing styles. They pose in front of the talus slope behind the camp.

Below:
A crew of woodsmen. This photo appears to be in camp somewhere.

Camp Rosario Beach

Above:
The leaders of the Rosario camp, most of them from the National Park Service.

Below:
948th Company men and officers, much of the entire camp standing on the talus slope as the sun gets low in the west.

Camp Rosario Beach

COMPANY ROSTER, 948th Company, C.C.C.
CAMP ROSARIO BEACH
Anacortes, Washington

ARMY PERSONNEL
Camp Commander—First Lieut Stephen C. Bacon, CA. RES.
First Lieut. Palmer A. Matthews, Eng., Res.
George B. Moore—Camp Surgeon
Frank L. Hatley—Educational Adviser

Senior Leader—Harold A. Olson
Company Clerk—Richard W. Maneval
Supply Steward—Eino E. Palo
Assistant Educational Adviser—Ed Elsassu
First Aid Attendant—Harry Thompson
Canteen Steward—Tom P. Gable
Camp Artificer—Telesphore L. Juneau

FORESTRY PERSONNEL
Camp Superintendent—Harry B. Buckley
L. Bowen   R. Carlson   P. Everett   J. O'Niel   C. Wiesse   L. DeFraine
K. Best   M. B. Crane   R. Koept   G. Hall   F. Fenton

MESS PERSONNEL
Lt. P. A. Matthews .... Mess Officer	Irvin H. Edwards .... Helper
O. D. Jackson .... Steward	Willard H. Eads .... Helper
D. W. Jackson .... Assistant	Fred J. Groves .... Helper
Lloyd Brooker .... First Cook	Robert W. Haley .... Helper
Clifford Casper .... First Cook	Sid M. Knowles .... Helper
V. Dee Lloyd Knowles .. Assistant Cook	Edward R. Perrault .... Helper
Harold A. Smith .... Assistant Cook	Al L. Welch .... Helper
Joe J. Belaich .... Baker	Edward W. Wissing .... Helper
Herbert H. Bates .... Helper	

Roster, All Members, the 948th Company, C.C.C., Nov. 30, 1934

LEADERS

Barney, Ernest W. ...CC9-137516 LEM	Drath, Ralph H. ....131691 JR
Conn, William C. ....131954 LEM	Hagan, Andrew P. ....131972 LEM
	Stearns, Clinton E. ....131962 LEM

ASSISTANT LEADERS

Eighme, Donald D. ....23587 LEM	Sollie, Ben ....117257 LEM
Gibson, Howard A. ....150336 LEM	Swift, Alvin W. ....131675 JR
McLeod, Boyd ....117253 LEM	Tobie, Bernard ....23544 LEM
Ogden, George N. ....131664 JR	Tucker, Harry V. ....16693 LEM
Rarey, William E. ....150338 LEM	Whalen, Henry B. ....135917 JR

MEMBERS

Allan, Wallace C. ....149558 JR	Bryson, Charles M. ....149059 JR
Allen, Harold J. ....150283 JR	Bust, Robert S. ....149060 JR
Anderson, Arvid N. ....151031 JR	Cameron, Alex J. ....CC9-150292 JR
Anthony, Donald R. ....134975 JR	Cameron, Nathan D. ....149061 JR
Armstrong, Harold F. ....150284 JR	Campau, John A. ....135906 JR
Arnestad, Clifford V. ....150285 JR	Campbell, James F. ....149559 JR
Atkins, Arnold J. ....150286 JR	Carpenter, Mae E. ....151788 JR
Ballew, Edward J. ....150748 JR	Cartee, James W. ....151228 LEM
Barker, William P. ....150287 JR	Congdon, Robert R. ....135904 JR
Barth, Robert F. ....131680 JR	Conine, Guy J. ....131685 JR
Beyers, John F. ....150289 JR	Conner, Don O. ....131686 JR
Bond, Archie W. ....150291 JR	Cornell, Francis D. ....134970 JR
Brooks, John A. ....150335 LEM	Cornish, Jesse R. ....151797 LEM
Brown, Winfield ....131291 JR	Coventry, Jack R. ....151789 JR
Brown, Wilbur D. ....135914 JR	Cox, Delburt F. ....131687 JR

ROSTER OF ALL MEMBERS—Continued

Crandall, Stanley E. ....131688 JR	McCollum, Harold O. ......150312 JR
Cunningham, Charles T. ....151787 JR	McDaniels, Hugh L. ......151235 LEM
Davis, William M. ......151229 LEM	McGilvery, Francis ......137270 JR
Dickson, Darrell A. ......151725 JR	McLaughlin, William G. ......150313 JR
Dimmick, Alton L. ......151790 JR	Mortvedt, Howard J. ......151043 JR
Durham, Leland N. ......151791 JR	Morris, Edwin A.
Eberhard, Oscar H. ......150293 JR	Myrick, James E. ......150316 JR
Eichholtz, Thomas S. ......131974 LEM	Niklason, Edward H. ......131967 LEM
Etherington, Leland C. ......131693 JR	Nordstrom, Chester A. ......134971 JR
Farmer, Fred A. ......131694 JR	Nyland, Charles R. ......131663 JR
Fitzgerald, George L. ......150295 JR	Olney, William G. ......131665 JR
Finney, Dick C. ......151037 JR	Osborn, Murel ......151728 JR
Flynn, Francis E. ......151038 JR	Ottesen, Frank V. ......150307 JR
Ford, Donald J. ......151792 JR	Pagh, Martin F. ......151722 JR
Foster, Tom B. ......131696 JR	Parrish, Zebedee W. ......150319 JR
Frazier, Henry J. ......149055 JR	Patterson, Tom U. ......131667 JR
Freeman, John V. ......151793 JR	Pearce, Sam L. ......135925 JR
Gamman, Roy B. ......150297 JR	Pegrum, Frank ......150308 JR
Gessner, Alvin C. ......150324 JR	Perecz, Lynn ......135903 JR
Ginnett, Albert V. ......150337 LEM	Perrault, Joe V. ......150318 JR
Gilreath, Jack K. ......131697 JR	Perry, Wayne L. ......150320 JR
Graham, Eugene J. ......150298 JR	Persson, Roy A. ......135902 JR
Granger, Melvin C. ......150299 JR	Phillips, Morton J. ......131234 LEM
Grant, Robert M. ......135923 JR	Phillips, Morton W. ......151234 LEM
Graves, Marx ......131656 JR	Pompella, Verne B. ......150321 JR
Gustavsen, Arthur ......151230 LEM	Prather, Eldon H. ......150322 JR
Haas, Edward B. ......150301 JR	Reed, Raynold B. ......149069 JR
Hagadorn, Albert ......150912 JR	Ringoen, Sylfest ......151729 LEM
Ingenum, Jack M. ......150302 JR	Robbins, Alfred F. ......131668 JR
Haley, Lincoln F. ......151232 LEM	Roberts, Carmon L. ......135919 JR
Hamilton, Joe H. ......151794 JR	Ronning, Harold O. ......150323 JR
Hansen, Hans C. ......135911 JR	Russell, Delvin F. ......150321 JR
Harris, John C. ......137516 LEM	Russell, James W. ......151236 LEM
Hauge, Elmer J. ......137269 JR	Schrader, Clyde S. ......151044 JR
Henley, Earl P. ......131659 JR	Schreindl, Alfred ......151795 JR
Henry, James C. ......151039 JR	Schwartz, Henry V. ......135901 JR
Hill, Lester ......23662 LEM	Severson, Albert C. ......150325 JR
Hill, Lewis J. ......150749 JR	Sexton, Frank W. ......131673 JR
Hill, Newton ......23588 LEM	Shaffer, Phillip M. ......150326 JR
Hoagland, Bill G. ......135910 JR	Shrewsbury, DeWitt T. ......150751 LEM
Hollenbeck, Edward W. ......149066 JR	Smith, James L. ......150309 JR
Irwin, Lewis P. ......131660 JR	Smith, Robert C. ......150327 JR
Isaksen, Roy F. ......150305 JR	Snyder, Frank F. ......131964 LEM
Jackson, Donald W. ......149557 JR	Spitzer, Lloyd C. ......151722 JR
Jelmberg, George O. ......131971 JR	Stevens, Phillip O. ......149056 LEM
Jenkins, Thomas R. ......134986 JR	Straub, Charlie W. ......117261 LEM
Johnson, Alve E. ......135920 JR	Stickles, Jack D. ......151796 JR
Johnson, Joseph B. ......150306 JR	Strowbridge, Justus P. ......150341 LEM
Kahn, Melvin C. ......134979 JR	Swan, Waldo L. ......150342 JR
Kellerman, Harold ......134978 JR	Templeton, Charles W. ......151726 JR
Kettleson, Chester S. ......151231 LEM	Thompson, Hugh G. ......135996 JR
Kensey, Rex B. ......151040 JR	Tripp, Claude A. ......134980 JR
Klaes, Howard J. ......151906 JR	Tschida, Leonard E. ......150329 JR
Knowles, Sid M. ......151041 JR	Turner, James R. ......137266 JR
Knudsen, Andrew W. ......151042 JR	Vannatter, Jess W. ......150330 JR
LaPlant, Albert P. ......136820 LEM	Walters, Frank T. G. ......151045 JR
Latham, Tod P. ......149066 JR	Weller, William O. ......150331 JR
Lavine, Harold ......151233 LEM	Wilson, Russell W. ......149072 JR
Lindstrom, C. Robert ......131668 JR	Wiltsey, Sims O. ......135809 JR
Loop, Kenneth D. ......151724 JR	Wire, Paul O. ......150333 JR
Lubach, Arthur E. ......150310 JR	Wissing, Edward W. J. ......135907 JR
Lundeberg, Walter C. ......150311 JR	Wood, Clarence F. ......131976 JR
Marzano, Albert D. ......137265 JR	Woods, Clarence J. ......150334 JR
Marzano, Joe A. ......137264 JR	Woyach, Peter W. ......151727 JR

HEADQUARTERS, 948th Company, C.C.C.

Rosario Beach Camp, SP-4   R.F.D. 2, Anacortes, Washington

Above:
A camp roster for Camp Rosario, November, 1934.

Left::
The drawing gives an accurate rendition of the camp, also taken from the perspective of the Cougar Gap area, but from further to the northwest.

ROSARIO BEACH

Truly one of the more magnificent settings in all of Washington State, Rosario Beach has dramatic and yet intimate scenery.

The rocks and tide pool areas are rich in marine life. The headland to the southwest is connected to the uplands by a narrow tombolo, a spit of land that is just above the highest of tides. The headland offers dramatic views in all directions.

Home to the Salish for centuries, Rosario holds special significance to local tribes.

The upland to the east is a naturally protected and level bench above the seashore.

Here the CCC built a kitchen shelter, a restroom, and a pump house for the well that pumped water to a cistern high on the hill between Rosario and Reservation Bay.

There may have been a bathhouse between the restroom and the beach called Sharpe's Cove on the south of the tombolo, but the earlier restroom no longer exists. The bathhouse apparently had a ladder leading from the uplands down the steep bank to the beach below. The waters of Rosario Strait are never warm, getting up to perhaps 12 degrees Celsius (53 degrees Fahrenheit) in summer, hardly inviting temperatures for swimming. The use of a bathhouse must have been minimal at best.

The pictures presented in the following pages show the construction of the kitchen shelter, attempts to build a pond in the marshy area below the kitchen shelter, and construction of the restroom, the parking lot and the entrance gate.

Rosario is a place that remains in the heart long after discovering its natural features and beauty. In 1983, the Salish Indian Nation placed a story pole about an ancestral maiden named Kokwalalwoot. Her story is told in display panels around the story pole, located on the tombolo. Her story celebrates the connection of our cultures with our environment in a meaningful way.

Our intentions will always be to protect and preserve these qualities in the landscape, much as the Salish remind us with their story, and the CCC did with their sensitive and restrained development in this area.

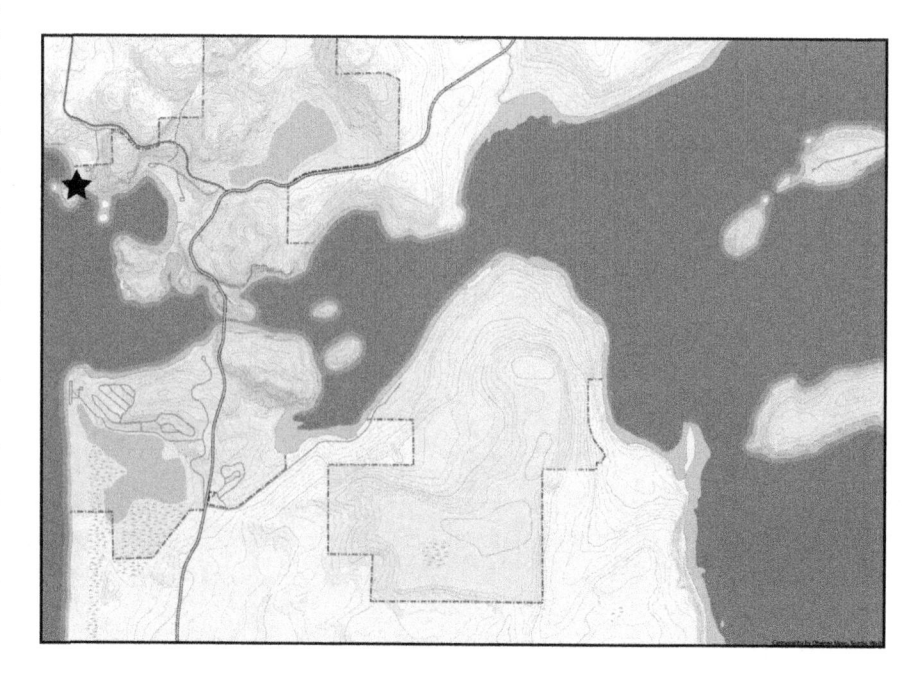

Rosario Beach

Above:
View of Rosario from the hillside rising north of Rosario Beach. View looking south. West Point and West Beach are above Rosario Head. Deception Island is partially hidden by the trees to the right. Deception Pass is out of sight to the left.

Rosario Beach

Above:
Clearing the parking area of trees, and stacking the firewood for use back at camp.

Below:
Men are splitting firewood on the left side of the picture. The large tree to the right of them is still there, with a distinctive hollow at its base. View of future parking area from location of current park restroom, looking west.

Rosario Beach

Above:
Dumping soil to build support for the parking lot where the trucks are currently sitting. Looking east across the west end of the parking lot, with the beach located behind the photographer.

Below:
The backshore between the beach and the kitchen shelter was a wetland of significant natural value. However, to the CCC in the thirties, it looked like an opportunity to build a wading pool. Here they use a wheelbarrow to remove native vegetation and dig the pool by hand.

Rosario Beach

Above:
Cleaning, deepening and widening the wetland to further develop the new pool. View is looking north from the east end of the tombolo toward what is now Walla Walla University's Marine Station. Various cabins climb the hill of what is still a residential community today.

Below:
Digging the pool deeper. Today, the area is again a backshore filled with drift logs and native vegetation.

Rosario Beach

Above:
The first structure to be built by the CCC at Rosario is the kitchen shelter. The ground was leveled, and the rock framework built up first.

Below:
With the rockwork done, the men could then raise the beams to support the roof. The rockwork at the Rosario shelter is very distinctive. When you visit, look at the patterns of extruded rocks in a wall of an otherwise uniform surface.

Rosario Beach

Above:
Now the rafters get raised, with the distinctive roof line designed by architect R. Koepf. This and the Reservation Bay shelters are the only shelters he designed at Deception Pass State Park.

Below:
Looking west at the newly built Rosario shelter. Rosario Bay can be seen through the windows. This shelter has a central stove area, with tables in a row on the water side. Photograph from the Washington State Digital Archives.

Rosario Beach

The finished Rosario kitchen shelter, overlooking the beach at Rosario. Notice the curved logs holding the beams at each entrance, and the extruded rocks of the foundation facing.

Photograph from the Washington State Digital Archives.

Rosario Beach

Above:
Detail of the stove rockwork at Rosario's shelter. From this view, the details of variety in the stonework can be seen, with occasional extruded rocks and distinctive patterns visible in the angles of the rocks.

Right:
From the inside of the shelter, looking south, showing the distinctive flair of the sweeping brace for the porch roof.

Both photographs from the Washington State Digital Archives.

Rosario Beach

Above:
After the kitchen shelter was finished, the crew began building a pump house for a water system to route water to Reservation Bay. Here, in the foreground, the pump house is just starting to get framed.
In the back left of the photo a bathhouse can be seen. Apparently built long before the CCC came here, it no longer exists.

Rosario Beach

Above:
The next building under construction is the restroom, around the corner from the kitchen shelter, near Sharpe's Cove on the south. The logs were shaped to fit each other with intricate notching. Compare this early picture with a finished picture in a couple of pages.

Below:
The men on the right are raising a heavy plate log on the 'latrine' at Rosario Beach. The vertical logs raised high above the building help in cabling the logs, which weigh thousands of pounds each, into their appropriate place.
The rockwork here continues the tradition of exuded rock on an otherwise smooth face, as seen in the shelter. View looking west toward Rosario Beach.

Rosario Beach

Above:
The restroom nearly completed, as the plumbing is installed. Note the hole in the ground on the right side of the restroom for the pipe installation. The man on the ladder takes care of details for the finish work.

Below:
The interior of the latrine is basic and plain as the plumbing gets installed. this area while still showcasing the original craftsmanship.

Rosario Beach

Above:
The finished restroom as seen from the east side. Note the distinctive light hanging to the left of the "MEN" sign. View looking southwest. Sharpe's Cove is on the left. Rosario Beach is off to the right.

This restroom was no longer used after the seventies, and sat mothballed for several decades until it was restored and renovated in 2011 to become a field classroom. The outside is still virtually identical to what it was when first built. The inside today is a beautiful open space for school groups to learn about the natural and cultural history of Rosario Beach and the Deception Pass area.

Rosario Beach

Above:
The same restroom at Rosario, as seen from the west, showing the Women's side. A trail to Reservation Bay begins to the right out of view of the camera.

Rosario Beach

Above:
The sign on the right side of the entrance gate to Rosario Beach. The font they chose for the lettering is certainly unusual. The letters were burned into the wood, making them stand out.

Both photographs from the Washington State Digital Archives.

Below:
The entrance to Rosario, with pillars standing on both sides. The left pillar says "Rosario Beach". The right pillar says "Deception Pass" facing traffic and "State Park" on the side as you enter. A low wall runs several meters to the left of the left column.

Rosario Beach

A closer view of the two gates, looking into the park. These signs were damaged and worn out after decades of Pacific Northwest weather. They were replaced with nearly exact replicas by volunteers in 2013.

Photograph from the Washington State Digital Archives.

Rosario Beach

Above:
Wind storms are one of the challenges of living in the Pacific Northwest along the Salish Sea. These trees have fallen northward in the parking lot, indicating it may have been a very strong southerly wind that knocked them over.
Notice the crosscut saw leaning against the standing tree, ready to be put to use to make something out of the downed wood.

Below:
The finished parking lot at Rosario, looking eastward toward the CCC camp which is out of sight behind the trees. The buildings of the private Rosario Beach Resort property can be seen beyond the parking lot on the left side of the picture. The resort eventually became the property of what is now Walla Walla University for use as a residential marine research laboratory.

Rosario Beach

Above:
And now Rosario Beach is again open for business.

Actually, the work is not yet finished, as evidenced by stakes in the ground in the right foreground, and railings still to be built. But it was a pretty spring day and people came to Rosario in droves.

The size of the parking lot determines how many people will be in this area at a given time. Limiting the size of the parking area limits the amount of resource damage that may ensue, and also allows visitors to have an experience in the area that is not dominated by human interaction. In this spirit, the parking lot has remained at about the same size as seen above.

Rosario Beach

Above:
The same day as the previous page, just a slightly different perspective, showing how many cars can fit in the parking lot. Of course, cars were smaller then.

In the background on the left side is an unknown building, not of CCC origin, that no longer exists.

"I first went to Rosario Beach and found at 1 pm. that every available parking space was taken. There was at that time one hundred and thirty two cars by actual count at that point. From there I went to Reservation Bay and found about me the same number on these grounds. I also found the kitchens in full use, and no surplus stoves anywhere."

—W. G. Weigle,
Superintendent, Washington State Parks,
letter dated June 27, 1936

RESERVATION BAY
(BOWMAN BAY)

A bay with two names. When it was a military reservation set aside as a defense base, the headland to the southwest was called Reservation Head, and the bay was called Reservation Bay.

Amos Bowman established a post office on the north side of Fidalgo Island in 1877, and named it "Anacortes," a play on the maiden name of his wife, Annie Curtis.

The Bowman family had many interests around Fidalgo Island, including this area. Eventually, the bay and the hill above were both named Bowman in honor of the family.

To the CCC, however, it was still called Reservation Bay, so all of the photographs refer to that name. We will use that name in this history of the CCC to identify the bay as they would have known it.

The CCC focused their efforts on the north end of the bay, building two shelters and a bathhouse with a restroom. They also built a caretaker's cabin and garage, and a smaller shelter a little farther to the south.

The CCC modified the natural wetlands at the south end of the bay, building two ditches across the marshland to create additional dry land, and building an outlet for Pass Creek that channeled the water into one creek exit rather than diffusing through the entire wetland.

In the late forties, the Washington Department of Fisheries built a fish hatchery at the south end of the bay, using fresh water from Pass Creek and the salt water of the bay to raise a variety of salmonids and other marine animals. They built numerous pens in the area that is now a playing field, and a duplex residence in the background to house hatchery staff.

They further modified the wetlands for the benefit of their hatchery operations, and built a wharf out into the bay to bring in salt water and supplies. And to protect these developments, they fortified the beach edge with a wall of rocks. A boat launch allowed park users to launch small craft to get into the bay and the waters beyond.

The hatchery became park land again in the early seventies. The tanks were smashed and buried to create a playfield. Everything else remains much as it was in the fifties.

Today's Bowman Bay looks nothing like what the original bay must have looked like when Salish peoples made this area their home. Maybe in the future, restoration of the shoreline can return some of the natural beauty and natural shore processes to the south side of the bay.

But overall, the charm and beauty of this area remain captivating.

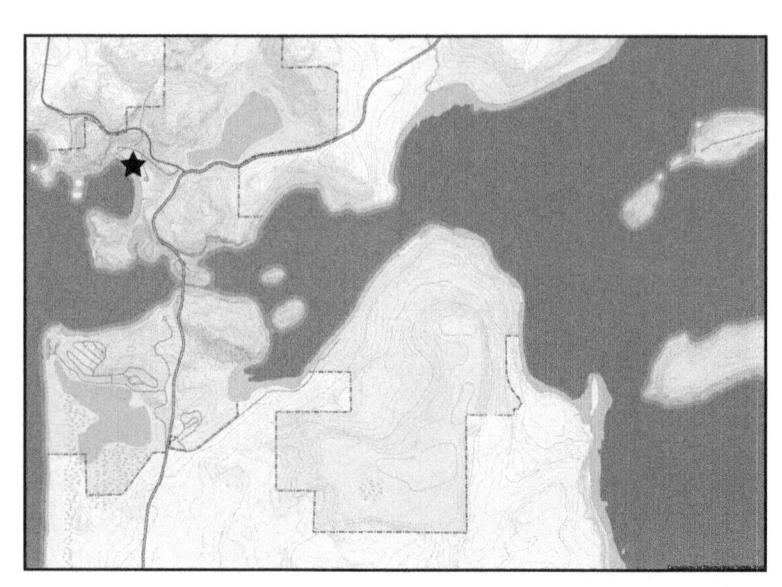

Reservation Bay

Above:

This and the next two photographs give a three-picture panorama of the north shore of Reservation Bay, now called Bowman Bay.

On this page, Rosario Head is at the entrance to the bay, with Coffin Rocks (left) and Gull Rocks (mid-left) exposed at low tide. Northwest Island can be seen between Rosario Head and the hill coming down from the right.

Photo taken from the headland just south of what is now the playfield at Bowman Bay.

Reservation Bay

Above:
The middle of the north shore of Reservation Bay, with Rosario Head out of view to the left, and the beach area out of view to the right. The reservoir for the water system that pumped water from Rosario to Reservation Bay facilities is high on the hill near the middle of the picture, though it is too small to be seen from here. View looking north from the north side of Reservation Head.

Below:
The beach of Reservation Bay. Bowman Hill rises in the distance in the right half of the picture. Pass Creek comes down the valley to the north (left) of Bowman Hill. Deception Pass is to the right of Bowman Hill.

Reservation Bay

Above:

Reservation Bay view taken from the headland south of the current playfield, looking north. The kitchen shelter at the beach and the bathhouse will be built in the field across the bay, just to the right of the large tree in the foreground.

In the thirties when this picture was taken, it appears that the area that is now a playfield was a marshy and woodsy area. This is where the drainage from Pass Lake reaches the sea. The shoreline of the bay is a gentle half-moon sweep from the far side of the picture down to the bottom of the picture.

Today, of course, the south portion of the bay has been modified to accommodate a fish hatchery years ago which remained until the seventies. The area now has a boat launch, parking lot, playfield, and duplex residence, protected by an artificial rock wall. Maybe someday we can say "tear down this wall" and it will happen.

Reservation Bay

Above:
Another view of the beach at Reservation Bay, this one taken from the trail that connects the bay with Rosario. The new shelter and bathhouse will be built by the CCC in the field near the left center of the picture.

Reservation Bay

Above:
Before the bridge was built, and even before the road down to Reservation Bay was built, this was about the only option for getting a vehicle into the worksite. The raft's origin is unknown, but it is landing at what is now the boat launch area.

The shelter in the background, built before the CCC era, would be replaced by a CCC-constructed shelter at about the same location.

Reservation Bay

Above:
Based on the volume of what appear to be alder trees, this scene is probably the south half of Reservation Bay, where CCC workers are creating a parking area out of the forest. It must have been a rainy time of the year.

Below:
The road from the previous picture is now staked and ready to be graveled. There is a drainage ditch in the foreground ready to have a culvert installed.
This view is apparently looking northward towards the present intersection of roads at Bowman Bay.

Reservation Bay

Above:
Building the road between Pass Lake and Reservation Bay. After the first cut through the woods, the debris is burned.

Below:
Now the laborious work of grubbing the roadway begins. It is all done by hand. Looking north down the new road bed heading toward Reservation Bay.

Reservation Bay

Above:
Digging by hand to create the road bed. The workers here are almost to the bottom of the hill near the intersection leading to either the boat launch or the campground today.

Next page:
The route from Pass Lake to Reservation Bay passes numerous outcroppings of bedrock, which must be blasted out or broken piece by piece with pick axe.

This rock is about halfway between the lake and the bay along the road, and creates a narrow pinch point even today.

Reservation Bay

Reservation Bay

Above:
Another view of the difficult rock area, about halfway down the road. This was slow and painful work.

Below:
The road crew is happy to take a break and pose for a picture at the rock outcropping. The tools visible in the picture are pointed shovels, sledge hammers, rock bars, and pick axes.

Reservation Bay

Above:
Another rock outcropping. The man on the hill chips away with his pick axe. Two others haul the rock debris away with wheel barrows.

Below:
The handwork continues. Progress was slow, but steady. Look at the fire scar on the tree on the right. This is a Douglas fir, which has thick bark and is able to resist most ground fires. This tree is still there today.

Reservation Bay

Above:
The road bed is nearly done now, with a thick layer of gravel on top. This bend in the road can be seen today, fairly close to the bottom of the roadway where it comes to an intersection. Note the care that the workers used to make the edge of the road blend with the forest environment quickly yet subtly.

Below:
This guardrail is similar to what was built at Rosario. It's exact location is not known, but it appears to be near the north end of the bay, not far from where the bathhouse will be located. The two CCC workers in front are trimming the end of the log to make a tight fit.

Reservation Bay

Above:
Two of the campsites in the new Reservation Bay campground. The tables and benches are handmade out of thick cedar. The waters of the bay can be seen off to the right.

The designs for CCC facilities always emphasized a separation of activities, with restrooms placed near parking lots, shelters placed separately near the beaches, and camping facilities off by themselves so that there would be no conflicting uses near to each other.

The present campground at Bowman Bay is very close to the beach-side kitchen shelter, causing us to wonder if the campsites illustrated above were to the south where no other development had occurred. The old growth timber would not easily fit that theory, however. This view is towards the south from the north end of the bay, presumably.

Reservation Bay

Above:
Construction of the beachside shelter begins. The kitchen is fitted upside down, then taken down and assembled in place. The walls and plate logs are shown here ready for construction.

The roof appears to be the roof from an earlier building before the CCC, here in place above the new rockwork frame of the beachside kitchen shelter.

The sign to the right cannot be read, but it seems to be a restrictive sign as the first word appears to be "No." Below it is another unreadable sign.

The bay is a short distance to the right in this photo looking southeast.

Reservation Bay

Above:
The finished kitchen shelter at Reservation Bay, with this view from the south. The windows of the shelter look out over the waters of Reservation Bay.

This design is considerably different from the other shelters in the park, other than Rosario, which was designed by the same architect. Notice the shingle siding above the south wall rockwork.

Photograph from the Washington State Digital Archives.

Reservation Bay

Above:
Another view of the beachside Reservation Bay shelter, looking at the south end of the building. The bay can be seen just beyond the building. The shelter appears to have overhead wires going into the building. These were later put underground.

Reservation Bay

Above:
The bathhouse at Bowman Bay, with the center station boarded up and not in use. View looking generally northerly, towards the modern campground. This bathhouse is larger than the one at East Cranberry Lake.

Notice the trees in the background have branches reaching all the way down to the ground. Today these trees have no branches near the ground, creating a more open feel to the lawn areas.

The bathhouse did not receive as much use as expected by the planners, probably because Reservation Bay does not get very warm for swimming. As the only restroom in the area at the time, however, it still served a valuable function.

Photograph from the Washington State Digital Archives.

Reservation Bay

Above:
A close-up of the bathhouse at Reservation Bay, looking at the right hand side, or the south side of the building, at the side that faces the bay. The door on the right enters the men's bathhouse and changing area. The door in back, under the light, is the men's restroom. The section on the left is the center section of the building, intended to be a service center and a concession sales area. CCC alumni converted the bathhouse into an interpretive center in 1988.

Photograph from the Washington State Digital Archives.

Reservation Bay

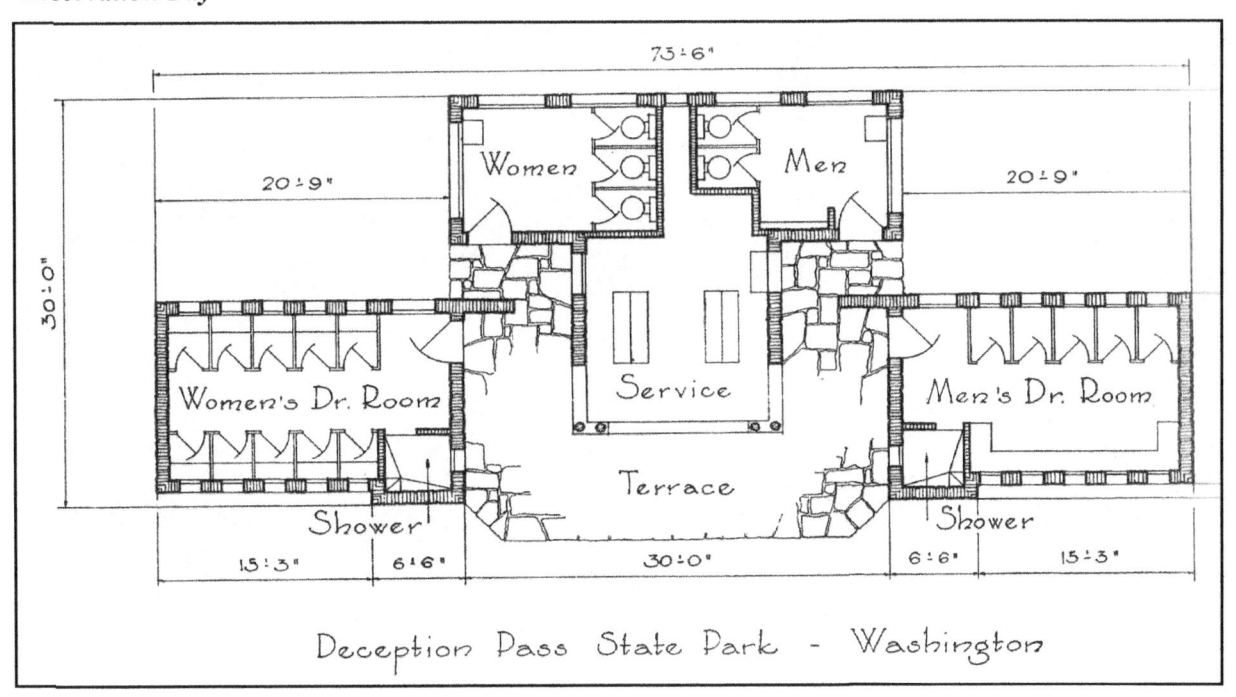

Above:

A sketch of the layout of the bathhouse at Reservation Bay.

A significant difference between this bathhouse and the one at East Cranberry is the addition of restrooms accessible to patrons of the bathhouse and those just needing a comfort station alone. Thus what might have been three or four smaller buildings are gathered into one common area.

Also, the dressing rooms are completely roofed here, and there are even showers provided, one on each side.

The question remained as to how many people would go swimming in the cold waters of Reservation Bay. The answer — not many. The building's lack of use made the decision easier decades later to convert it into an interpretive center.

Drawing courtesy of Albert H. Good

Reservation Bay

Above:
A very small shelter built south of the rest of the developments at Reservation Bay, just north of the modern day parking lot at the boat launch. It is too small to even put a table under the shelter, having just enough room for the stove.

Around 2008, the posts had to be replaced due to wood rot at the ground level. Most of the CCC structures were designed to have beams, posts, and other critical components exposed to the elements, providing several future opportunities for failure if not repaired.

Photograph from the Washington State Digital Archives.

Reservation Bay

Above:
At the south end of Reservation Bay, the outlet of Pass Lake creates a wetland behind the beach, and eventually enters the bay. The trail to Lighthouse Point crosses this creek, requiring a bridge to keep hikers' feet dry.

Above:
Bare-chested workers build the forms for the foundation of the new bridge. View looking northward.

Below:
The crew pours the footings into the molds they created. View looking southeast.

Reservation Bay

Above:
Cedar stringers are built into granite abutments of the bridge. The footings can be seen below them. The outlet was dry this time of year, but has a steady sizeable stream when the wet season returns.

Photo looking eastward towards the wetland.

Below:
The footbridge is completed, with a handsome appearance. Notice the rock bulkhead built around the footings to hide the framework, and to add protection from wave action and the erosion effects of the outlet.

Reservation Bay

The view from just outside the Reservation Bay kitchen shelter, looking southwest toward Deception Island.

The three signs on the left of the sign post point to Lighthouse Point, Canoe Pass, and Pass Lake. The sign pointing right says Rosario Beach. On the post itself, written vertically, the name Reservation Bay has been carved into it.

Photograph from the Washington State Digital Archives.

Following pages:
Park planners wanted to have a caretaker cabin built near the intersection of the Reservation Bay road, where it splits to go north to the shelters or south to the boat launch. This would allow a caretaker to theoretically be aware of every vehicle entering the Reservation Bay area.

The following section of photographs depict the construction of the cabin, and the garage built next door. Set on the side of the hill looking over the bay, this cabin is still a remarkable synergy of beauty, craftsmanship, and purpose.

Reservation Bay

Above:
Logs for the caretaker's cabin were first brought to Reservation Bay by raft from Hoypus Point. They were stored in the parking area that had been built on the south side of the developed part of the bay, then peeled and prepared for hauling the final two hundred meters to the construction site.

Below:
Enrollees hook the logs to a skidder to haul them up 100 meters to the location of the new cabin.

Reservation Bay

Above:
Some of the logs were rough cut while still at the loading zone for preparation for use at the cabin, then hauled by the truck up to the cabin site.

Below:
Workers dig the basement of the caretaker's cabin by hand, excavating material to be used later for surfacing the picnic area.

Reservation Bay

Above:
Sand for mortar was obtained from the beach. Using the screen shown here, workers washed the sand for twenty minutes to remove the salt, then loaded it into the truck to be hauled to the home site.

Below:
The framework is going up for building the masonry wall of the cabin. Looking northwest towards the parking lot and present day campground area. Crew members dug the foundation with pick and shovel in August of 1934.

Reservation Bay

Above:
The basement begins to take shape. They gathered the granite for the foundation in the park and cut it on location. The bay can be seen in the far left of the picture, just beyond the parking area.

Below:
Looking north, the walls of the basement and ground level are rising.

Reservation Bay

With the basement walls fabricated, the logs for the cabin are now being fitted, outlining the shape of the cabin.

Craftsmanship is required at every step of the process. They fitted each log one by one, as each log had a unique shape requiring detailed handwork. The logs also had to be constructed in such a way as to allow for settlement as they dried out. The door frames had to be fitted and tacked so that the logs could slide past the frames as the logs settled.

Reservation Bay

Above:
The first roof is placed on the caretaker's cabin. In the foreground, the rock foundation of the garage has been built, and is ready for the logs as well.

Below:
The caretaker's cabin is completed, including the basic landscaping in the yard. This side of the house faces the water of the bay. The garage is being built to the right of the picture.

167

Reservation Bay

The front entrance of the house, showing the detail of the porch, the roof lines, and the log construction. Rockwork is mostly in the basement of the house.

The CCC directors only allowed $1,400 to be spent on materials for the house, and $600 for specialized labor. Ellsworth Storey designed the building along with many other structures in the area. Kirk Best was the foreman in charge of the project.

Because of the slope of the ground, very little masonry is above the ground on the uphill side, leading to maintenance problems many decades later with the bottom logs being exposed to ground moisture.

Photograph from the Washington State Digital Archives.

Reservation Bay

Above:
Another view of the front of the house, showing more of the kitchen area to the right. Harry Buckley, camp superintendent in 1935, and his wife Esther had the privilege of being the first occupants of the house. The caretaker's house has been continuously occupied ever since it was finished in 1935. With dozens of families calling this house their home over the years, it is remarkable that it still appears nearly identical to how it looked 80 years ago.

Left:
The structural details of the side entrance, with the kitchen to the left of the door. This house is nearly identical to the caretaker's cabin near the old entrance on the Whidbey Island side of the bridge, but turned 180 degrees, having the front door facing south, and the view windows of the living room facing the water. This door faces east.

Photograph from the Washington State Digital Archives.

Reservation Bay

The interior of the house, showing the remarkable beams and log walls in the living room, and the fireplace dominating the left wall.

The Buckleys suggested naming the cabin "The Big Moon of Feasting," as "the moonlight is so beautiful through the windows and on the grounds around the house at night."

Compare this picture with the interior photograph of the caretaker's cabin near the old entrance (page 75) when it is set up for a dinner.

Reservation Bay

Above:
Workers using pick axes and shovels grading the site for the caretaker's garage, just south of the cabin. Building materials are on hand for construction.

Below:
The finished garage, this photo taken a few years later after vegetation has become established around the structure, maybe inappropriately. The hemlock growing under the first window of the workshop will cause problems very soon.

Reservation Bay

Above:

The garage and workshop building are both now completed. The door on the left leads to a workshop, the only work space for park staff on this side of the bridge at the time. The two bays are for the caretaker and for park maintenance equipment and vehicles.

The cabin is behind the photographer and to the left.

Note that the color of the wood is a natural wood grain finish. It was only in later decades that a chocolate stain or paint was added to CCC buildings, significantly altering their appearance and character.

Photograph from the Washington State Digital Archives.

BUILDING THE HIGHWAY
FIDALGO ISLAND SIDE

For many decades before the CCC, Fidalgo Island had a network of roads connecting its hamlets and communities. The Rosario Beach area connected to Dewey Beach, formerly known as Fidalgo City, via a meandering roadway along the north shore of Pass Lake. A prison camp worked the cliffs between Dewey Beach and Deception Pass around 1910, bringing in further need for roads and services.

But nothing, not even way trails, penetrated the thick woods and steep terrain at the southwest tip of Fidalgo Island, where a new bridge was going to be built. The bare rock faces dropped precipitously a hundred meters or more to the swift waters of Deception Pass below.

CCC Camp Rosario Beach had a challenge. It was their job to build the roadway connecting this new bridge site on the side of a cliff with the town of Dewey Beach, and thus to Anacortes and the mainland to the east.

Not only did they face the challenging terrain of the pass area itself, the shoreline of Pass Lake was also a menacing problem, with similar rock faces descending directly into the lake and no level place that was apparent to build a thoroughfare for a major highway.

Armed with hand tools and a little dynamite, the Corps members got to work, blasting and cutting and hacking their way through these obstacles to create a scenic route that is now taken for granted.

This section looks at the creation of that highway, starting at Pass Lake and culminating in the climb to the edge of the cliff where the new bridge would soon cross over to Whidbey Island, bringing direct driving access to the island for the first time ever.

It still remains the only vehicle access route to Whidbey Island that does not require a boat.

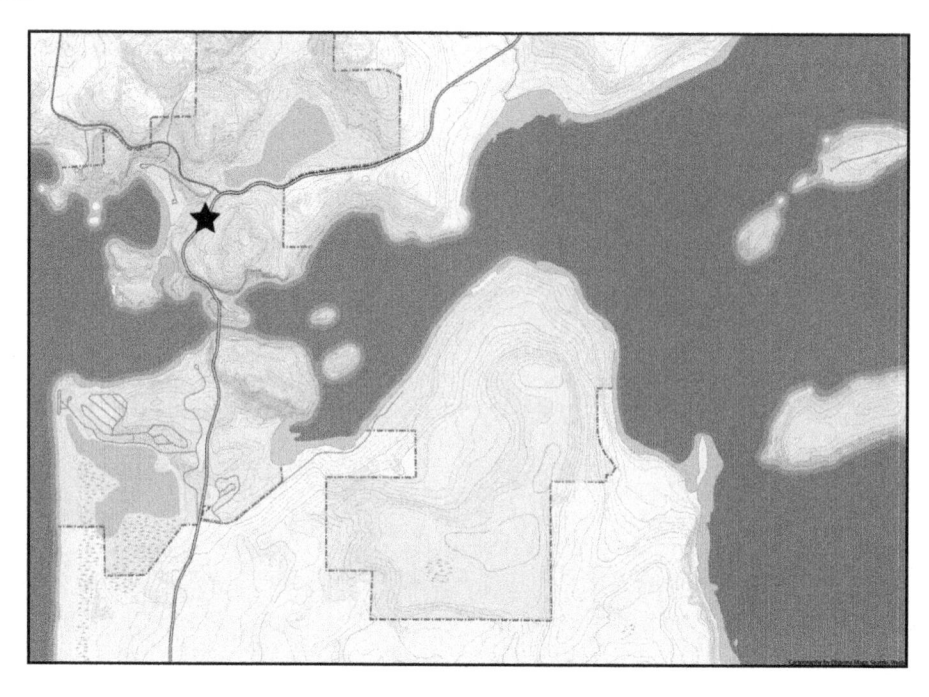

Highway 20, Fidalgo Side

Above:
The proposed highway to Deception Pass crossed two small lagoons on Pass Lake, necessitating floating trails. Cliffs along the shore also required precarious foot travel to safely navigate around the lake. Here is where they were to build a road, a two-lane highway.

Below:
The steep forested walls of Bowman Hill came right down to the water's edge along Pass Lake.

Highway 20, Fidalgo Side

Photos taken in almost the identical place along the southwest shore of Pass Lake. The left picture was taken before the roadbed was built, showing the challenging terrain. The below picture was taken after the roadbed is complete. The guardrail will be added later.

Highway 20, Fidalgo Side

Trees along the edge of the lake have been cut in a few places as the crew begins the process of clearing the roadway. Firewood is stacked on the far left side of the picture.

View looking west, toward the outlet.

Highway 20, Fidalgo Side

Above:
The southwest shore, about 400 meters east of the previous picture, looking west. The point on the right getting cleared out is at about milepost 43 today.

Below:
Photo taken in almost the identical place as the previous picture, only now the roadbed is completed. The guardrail will be added later.

Next page:
The road bed nearly finished, with guardrails.

Highway 20, Fidalgo Side

Highway 20, Fidalgo Side

After leaving the challenges of Pass Lake, the crews immediately encountered their next problem: large trees, large rocks, and extremely steep slopes. Building a trail through here would be a battle, let alone a highway.

Boulders the size of cars, thick trees, and a hillside that slopes severely and falls down to the water's edge: these are some of the obstacles facing the road building crew. Lost in the blur of motion, there is a CCC worker using some small power equipment to fell the large Douglas fir now lying on the ground on the slope. His fellow Corps member stands with a peavey to help move logs out of the way — if he can.

Highway 20, Fidalgo Side

More examples of the work they performed as they cut a route up the hill to the pass. Consider how many trees were dropped and removed to be used elsewhere. And then consider that they had to level this route using picks, shovels, and rakes — they must have slept well at night.

It is hard to imagine dropping a tree as large as the one, using only a crosscut saw pulled back and forth by two men.

Highway 20, Fidalgo Side

Above:
A "before" picture, showing the tangle of large standing and downed trees that had to be removed, and the steep terrain that had to be negotiated and leveled.

Below:
After much cutting, and removing usable wood for projects elsewhere, the slash debris is burned in preparation of the contour work on the road bed itself.

Highway 20, Fidalgo Side

Two pictures of the same area, showing the rocks and trees removed after cutting trees and blasting rock and stumps.

Highway 20, Fidalgo Side

Above:
This picture is labeled "the compressor gets going on Deception Pass Highway."

Below:
After clearing the road of trees and bedrock, the roadbed begins to take shape. Notice once again that nothing goes to waste: firewood is stacked neatly on the left side of the picture, ready for future use.

Highway 20, Fidalgo Side

Above:
Imagine trying to build a roadway across this hillside. The men of the CCC did just that. This is the location of the large turnout on the highway, just before the bridge on the north side of the pass. It looks so different now.
View looking southeast, with Pass Island in the middle distance and Goose Rock on Whidbey Island in the background.

Highway 20, Fidalgo Side

Above:
A similar view as the previous page, after some further clearing work has been done. The top of Goose Rock is visible in the background. The waters of Deception Pass swirl over 50 meters below here.

Highway 20, Fidalgo Side

Above:
Getting closer to the cliff's edge in this view. Pass Island and the northern end of Whidbey Island are easy to see from here. You can also see the progress taking place on the Whidbey side. The rock debris is the aftermath of a large blast of dynamite breaking up the rock face into pieces that the CCC workers can now remove.

Highway 20, Fidalgo Side

Above:
Blasting through the rock hillside created debris that cascaded down the edge of the cliffs to the water below, changing the environment of the slopes and the shoreline. This debris eventually gathered soil and allowed trees to grow in the area near the highway, trees which eventually grew tall enough to block the view of what used to be a dramatic and open panorama of the bridge area and pass. The original landscape never had many sizeable trees in this area.

Current management practices mitigate the loss of view with judicious and thoughtful pruning.

Highway 20, Fidalgo Side

Above:
While the roadway is being built, the bridge itself is also underway. In this stunning view, the north approach is under construction, Pass Island is in the middle, and work can now clearly be seen on the Whidbey side as well.

Photograph from the Washington State Digital Archives.

Highway 20, Fidalgo Side

Above:
The location of this picture is unknown. CCC men place loose rocks, creating a wall to hold the toe of the fill slope.

Below:
Twelve feet of fill material was added to this area. Now the slopes are stabilized and planted.

Highway 20, Fidalgo Side

Above:
Having powered equipment makes work much easier. Here a dump truck is used as a 'cherry picker' to place guardrails onto the rock supports along the edge of the highway.

Highway 20, Fidalgo Side

Above:
A completed section of road and railing north of the bridge, where the highway makes a sharp turn to the right northbound. View is looking northeast, with Pass Lake around the bend in the distance. The rock columns are made of local basalt rock according to the photograph's notes, spaced eighteen feet apart. The logs are sixteen feet long, with a diameter of fourteen to sixteen inches.

Highway 20, Fidalgo Side

Above:
Looking back towards the spot where the picture on the previous page was taken from, where the road turns left in the distance. The bridge is around the corner up ahead.

It appears that some kind of construction sheds were built at the corner up ahead, temporary structures that are no longer there, although the highway does have a small turnout at that corner.

Highway 20, Fidalgo Side

Above:

One of the rock supports for the highway railings, showing the basalt rock put together with intricate precision. The two shoulders, one on each side of the column, have a large pin embedded within. The log has a vertical hole drilled on its bottom side to accept the pin, holding the log in place. This pin is the only counterforce for stopping a vehicle if it hits the log.

The two CCC camps built their rock columns differently, reflecting different local experienced men helping each camp with this project. Columns on the north side of the bridge, like the one shown here, have a mortar cap on top. The columns on the south side usually do not.

Highway 20, Fidalgo Side

Above:
A newspaper photograph showing a group of CCC men building the railing on the north side of the bridge, about two hundred meters from the bridge. The waters of Deception Pass are lost in the graininess of the picture beyond the trees. The logs and rock columns in this area were all replaced when the new guardrails were built here in 2008.

INFRASTRUCTURE

Buildings and roadways stand out as megastructures, facilities that we see because of their size, their presence in the landscape, and their usefulness. We become more attentive to the details of a shelter as we use it. We see the forms of buildings, the heavy weight of the rocks and logs, the architectural lines of the walls and roof. Roadways cut wide swaths through the woods, opening routes of travel and newly appearing vistas as we travel their courses.

Just as useful, but often completely unseen, are the infrastructural elements that make the buildings and landscapes actually work: the water lines, the sewer lines, the power lines, and the other detailed work that goes into the basic elements of a park system.

These elements are not the subject of table talk, or photo books, or travel guides. But without them, the rest of the projects would be impossible.

Water lines fed the residences, restrooms, and shelters, often from creative sources. Sewer lines and septic tanks accompany every occupied facility in the park. Drain lines take surface water away from buildings. Stonework allows stoves and walls to be built. Telephone lines connect buildings for communication. And someone had to plan where everything went, meaning surveyors laid all these details out on a map before the physical work could take place.

All of these tasks were captured in photographs, and are shared here to honor this work and acknowledge the details that keep this park functioning.

Infrastructure

Above:
Beginning the North Beach septic field, downstream from the restroom there.

Below:
The septic tank is ready to pour. Bags of concrete, a wheelbarrow, and a mixing machine are the tools of trade for the concrete workers.

Infrastructure

Above:
Making the forms for a concrete water storage tank. These are some of the details that remain out of sight in the park, yet are integral to the work of the CCC in creating a functioning park.

Below:
It takes a large and diverse crew to create a water or sewer system. The jobs that need to be done include clearing the field, digging the lines, installing the tank, plumbing the connections, double-checking gradients, and making sure it all works.

Infrastructure

Above:
Before backhoes and power trenchers, the CCC men used strong backs and sharp pick axes to dig water lines. Miles of water lines were buried throughout the park.

Below:
A crew is putting the pipes into a water line dug alongside a roadway in the park. These water line routes are still in use, with more modern piping replacing the original lines as they wear out.

Following pages:
More lines being laid throughout the park.

Infrastructure

Infrastructure

Infrastructure

Above:
And yet more lines. This picture may be at the Cornet Bay Camp, looking south.

Below:
Shovels to the ready as more digging is in store.

Infrastructure

Above:
Mixing the concrete for the 10,000 gallon reinforced concrete reservoir, high on the hill between Rosario and Reservation Bay.

View looking southwest.

Right:
The completed reservoir. The building is mostly just a roof for the cistern, less than six feet higher than the ground. Remnants of the structure remain in the park to this day.

View looking eastward.

Infrastructure

Above:
Laying the pipeline between Rosario and Reservation Bay, barely visible in the background. Consider the effort it took to dig a pipeline through the hillside between these two locations. This engineering and physical accomplishment is astounding.

Infrastructure

Above:
From Pass Lake, another water or drain line was laid from the outlet of the lake to Reservation Bay. Here the pipes are fitted together at the lakeshore.

View looking east from near the present-day Pass Lake parking area.

Infrastructure

Above:
This appears to be taken just a short distance from the picture on the previous page, as workers dig a line from the lakeshore down to Reservation Bay. Almost everyone is wearing their oil raincoats and hats, and the trees are bare of leaves, so it must be a rainy day in winter.

Below:
Further down the hill, following the path of Pass Creek, the crew is placing a twenty-four-inch corrugated iron culvert.

Infrastructure

A crew builds a drain line to take water away from a recreation area and allow the ground to become drier. Picture taken at Rosario.

Infrastructure

Stringing telephone line on a pole. Picture taken on the Whidbey side of the park, unknown location.

Infrastructure

Above:
The laborious work of splitting granite for building foundations.

Below:
A crew working on the granite to create the rocks shaped just right to fit into a foundation wall for a park building, or a kitchen stove. All of the stone masonry was installed to be harmonious with the natural environment with freehand lines, rough cut stone, and strict avoidance of straight lines and angles. They used random patterns of stone placement, a variety of colors, weathered surfaces, deep mortar joints, and no parallel joints on the top course, emphasizing the design principles and the skilled craftsmanship of this era.

Infrastructure

Left:
Somewhere on the Whidbey side this stove was built out of the granite rocks, but no building appears to be in need of it. The stove just sits by itself somewhere.

Below:
Two proud enrollees, congratulating each other for a job well done. The distinctive rockwork will be easy to recognize if it can be found.

"For another 4 or 5 weeks I prepared the rock for the buildings. We'd bring big slabs into the site where we were building the buildings and we'd break them into whatever we needed. We'd take a cold chisel, beat it, score it, then break off whatever size they wanted."

—Milsen Kellner

Infrastructure

Above:
"Snag felled by tree hazard removal crew." Picture taken on the Whidbey side of old growth timber that had to be cut because of the fire hazard it represented. It takes a large crew to fell a tree of this size, over six feet in diameter.

Below:
Crews busy splitting wood for the kitchen. Keeping the stoves burning took a vast quantity of timber.

Infrastructure

Above:
The photo is labeled "CCC logging company," which is as good a description as any. Many trees were harvested in the Hoypus Point area for use in the rest of the park. There is even a trail at Hoypus Point called the "CCC Crossing".

The question is, though: How did they get that log up that ramp?

Below:
Somehow they did.

Infrastructure

Above:
Another crew, another full load of just three logs. The crew sits proudly in front.

Below:
Cutting cedar on West Beach, using a crosscut saw to bring back portions of the logs that can be split for shakes.

"We had an old time faller... and his biggest job was to try to keep us from killing ourselves. But we made our own springboards and he taught us how to use the tools."

—Don Olson

Infrastructure

Above:
Hand-splitting individual cedar shakes out of bolts of wood. The gentleman on the left holds a froe to split the shakes when hit by a mallet. The man fourth from left holds a sledge hammer, it appears, and a wedge.

The crew members hand split all of the shakes for the roofs in the park, covering thousands of square feet of roof one shake at a time.

Below:
Piles of thirty-six inch or forty-two inch shakes, or both, on the left side of the photo, with raw material on the right.

Infrastructure

Above:
A survey crew on a beach somewhere in the park, measuring elevations and control points. Location unknown.

Right:
A close-up of the survey crew.

ROADWAYS

Several of the National Park Service photographs capture the development of roadways throughout Deception Pass State Park. Most of these were highlighted in the Reservation Bay section of this book as the CCC built a roadway between Pass Lake and the facilities at the bay.

A handful of photographs leave us guessing as to where they were taken in the park. They are included here because they show aspects of road construction illustrated nowhere else in this book, and rarely seen or remembered at all anymore.

As the Cultural Resources Plan for the park states, roads were integral to a park visitor's experience. Roads controlled visitor access to services, as well as to views and vistas, and represented the primary man-made intrusion on the natural landscape.

Roads were conceived not only as a basic means of access, but also as a primary tool in the larger goal of defining and improving the visitor experience.

NPS Landscape Architect Daniel Hull stressed that the design of roads should aim for maximum scenic vantage points. Monotony was to be avoided, through transitions in vegetation, light, shade, and view. Curves, blending road cuts into natural topography, and revegetating scars created by construction became part of standard road design and development.

Roadways built by the CCC throughout Deception Pass reflect these design principles, with easy flowing curves, scenic overlooks, and a sensitivity to the natural surroundings and the needs of the park visitor.

The CCC formed rounded and flattened slopes next to the roads to reduce erosion and visually blend the disturbed ground into the natural areas. They even took the effort to use irregular tree lines at the clearing edges of roads to reduce the man-made look of roadways.

Planners even considered the safety and circulation of visitors through the south side of the park by building an underpass beneath Highway 20 so that each visitor who entered the park at the main entrance could visit every part of the park without having to face the traffic of the highway.

The closer we look at the work of the CCC and the designs they were following, the more we appreciate the care and attention they gave to complement the remarkable natural environment they were given to develop. That their developments seem like a natural part of the landscape is a testament to their design concepts and their workmanship carrying out these concepts for something as commonplace as a roadway.

Roadways

Left:
Mining gravel with a steam shovel to create the base of a roadway.

Below:
The set-up for crushing rocks for park roads, mining the rocks from the hillside, then crushing them in the make-shift grinder, then hauling them to the next section of road to be built.

Roadways

Above:
Making a twelve-foot fill with a drag scraper towed behind a #50 caterpillar tractor. As usual, downed trees are cut into firewood, seen on the right, for use in the kitchen stoves. Location unknown.

Below:
This bank provides an excellent supply of surfacing material for roads and parking areas. This may have been taken near Hoypus Point.

Roadways

Above:
A twenty foot rock wall with fifteen hundred cubic meters of fill. This wall can be found below Highway 20, just north of the bridge, facing the water.

Below:
Steam shovel work making the creation of the road bed a little easier than digging by hand.

Roadways

Above:
Laying course material for a base to a new road, which is then being raked by hand by the men standing to each side.

Below:
A curve in a park road, with the final grading in place. Roadways in the thirties were built for the narrow vehicles of the time. Today's wider rigs make some of these roadways a tight fit when two cars pass. Some of the roads are not wide enough to have a fog line painted on the sides as the roads are not the minimum width for each lane. This requires park traffic to travel slower, which is a good idea in a park for many reasons.

Roadways

Left: The road roughed in between Cornet Bay and North Beach.

Roadways

Left:
An unknown roadway in the park softened with white in the winter.

Roadways

Left:
A curve in a new park road. The narrowness of the roadway was appropriate for narrower cars driven at slower speeds. Routing roadways around significant old growth trees gave heightened awareness of the beauty all around. This roadway is on the south side of the bridge somewhere in the interior of the park.

Roadways

Left:
Another roadway under construction, winding, narrow, and sensitive to the landscape.

Photograph from the Washington State Digital Archives.

TRAILS AND SIGNPOSTS

Trails and signposts might be some of the most iconic CCC elements that people think of when visiting a park like Deception Pass. Period-appropriate lettering carved into wood with careful craftsmanship focused on each letter says "CCC." Seeing the sign next to a trail that wanders the woodlands beyond puts any one of us back into the feeling of a long ago era, when travel by foot was common and adventures awaited around each new bend of a trail.

The pictures in this section start on the Whidbey side, with photos of North Beach, West Beach, Cranberry Lake, Goose Rock, and the Hoypus Point area. The photos then look at trails at Reservation Bay and Rosario, followed by some classic photos of signs, some on trails, some beside roadways.

Many of today's trails still show the evidence of the rockwork or other details that the CCC men created as they built pathways through the park.

One concern about the trails in Deception Pass State Park is how they seem to be routed near cliffs and other potentially dangerous locations. Part of the challenge of any park, but particularly here, is to allow visitors to enjoy the dramatic landscapes without putting them into unduly hazardous terrain.

Parks are places where we want to give visitors the freedom to explore nature and wild lands. Sometimes that exploration can lead to places that require skill and common sense to navigate the pathways and return safely home again.

Should we remove all hazards by building people-proof fences along every trail and cliff? Should we trust visitors to understand the dangers and act accordingly?

We cannot fence off every cliff edge or high rock in the park. The freedom to experience a park on its own terms also carries the potential to get hurt if careless. We tend not to build trails on the edge of a cliff without building a fence or giving adequate warning through signage or other management tool.

But hazardous areas remain, and visitors must be aware of the danger, and take personal responsibility for their actions when they choose to experience the untamed wild at our doorstep.

The trails built by the CCC took visitors to high points, cliff edges, and deep forest woodlands. The photos ahead show the wide variety of landscapes at Deception Pass.

Trails and Signposts

Above:
A winding switchback trail reported to be the trail down to North Beach from the bridge before the CCC began their trail work.

Right:
To eliminate the switchbacks, a rock wall had to be built into the hillside, holding the trail bed in place. This wall is still visible just west of the bridge on the North Beach Trail.

Trails and Signposts

Left:
Work on the rock wall on the uphill side of the trail. The highway is at the top of the hill, leading to the bridge.

View facing south.

Below:
More of the rock-facing work on the uphill side of the trail. A ramp has been built to bring materials from the top.

View facing north.

Trails and Signposts

Above:
A dry rock retaining wall built on the trail from the bridge to North Beach.

Below:
From the North Beach parking area down to Little North Beach, this rock wall held the bottom end of the trail.

Trails and Signposts

Left:
A trail still needing to be smoothed out for the finished look.

Trails and Signposts

Left:
A fire burns behind the workers as they smooth out the final touches on the trail.

Trails and Signposts

Left:
A trail through the woods.

Trails and Signposts

Left:
This finished trail looks as if it had always been a part of the forest.

Trails and Signposts

Left:
Building a section of trail through the woods near the west end of North Beach.

Trails and Signposts

Above:
The finished trail winds through the woods above North Beach with numerous views out over the beach and Deception Pass.

Below:
Probably located at the base of the North Beach trail that leads to the bridge, this sign says "1/8 mile" on the left of the post, and Bridge Point on the right, pointing to the trail leading to the bridge. Below it is the trail name, Goose Rock Trail, which at the time this photo was taken would have been the name of the trail, as there was no parking lot yet to serve as a starting point for hikers to Goose Rock.

Trails and Signposts

Above:

An intriguing sign. Created out of the base of a tree, the words "North Beach Area" are burned into the wood vertically, showing that this sign was the main directional sign for North Beach.

The top sign on the left points to "Cranberry Lake Road," the road that descends sharply to get to North Beach. The other two signs on the left point down the trail to West Point and Cranberry Lake, almost a mile away.

The top right sign points to the trail to the right and says "Gun Point." Below it and pointing the same way is a sign, half hidden, that says "North Beach Kitchen."

Between those two signs, pointing behind and to the right of the photographer, the sign says only "Kitchen." The sign pointing almost into the camera is unreadable, but it has two short words that may say "Bridge Point." (See previous photograph.)

Curiously, there appears to be a building in the woods to the left. It could be the larger shelter at North Beach, but this is not clear. The roof angle appears to be different, and there is a lot of vegetation around it as well. Where the restroom is in relation to this sign is a good mystery. This area is obviously well traveled, a busy intersection of trails.

Trails and Signposts

Above:
A bench built into a signpost at a junction between several trails. Native materials help maintain a natural, park-like look. With the left two signs pointing east towards Cornet Bay and Goose Rock, and the right sign pointing north to North Beach, this sign may have been located somewhere near the underpass.

Trails and Signposts

Two North Beach trail views, the trail on the left going through a mossy outcropping area, the trail on the next page through a scenic old-growth forest glade.

Trails and Signposts

Trails and Signposts

Above:
A section of the North Beach Trail.

Next page:
The Cranberry Lake Trail meandering along the side of the lake. This is now roadway.

Trails and Signposts

Trails and Signposts

Left:
A sign not built to CCC standards, using two pieces of driftwood bolted together, but the worker seems to be proud of it regardless. The sign says "To Goose Rock Trail." The location is unknown. But it is creative.

Below:
A bench built into the side of the hill on the Goose Rock trail, somewhere above the new highway but some distance below the summit.

Trails and Signposts

Above:
This bridge looks like a simple solution for a simple problem. Logs or other obstacles appear to be blocking a straight bridge, so there is a minor jog in the middle of the bridge. The shallow nature of the depression means no serious consequence if you fail to negotiate the jog.

Below:
Same concept, but a more critical location. Could someone have really designed this? Did this make sense on paper, maybe? Did no one say "Wait a minute — what if…?"

Both pictures are of bridges in the North Beach area. Neither still exist, fortunately.

Trails and Signposts

Above:
Before West Beach was a parking lot, it was a natural beach. This sign and bench appear to be in the vicinity of the middle of the present parking lot, with the "Hilltop" restroom now built among the trees on the right in the background. Signs say "Strait of Juan de Fuca" on the far left; below that is an unreadable sign pointing north, and a sign below saying "North Beach Kitchens." On the right it says "Sand Dunes" and "Cranberry Lake Trail."

Next page:
A trail built along the East Boundary Fire Line. This may be what is now called the Fireside Trail, running east-west in the middle of the Hoypus Hill area.

Trails and Signposts

Trails and Signposts

Trails and Signposts

Previous page:
Another East Boundary Trail view, somewhere on Hoypus. Hoypus has a variety of environments, some logged previously, some old growth timber. Here is a young stand of alder.

Above:
The Hoypus Point Fire Trail. Hoypus Point provided much of the timber that now comprises the log buildings in the park. Logs were cut here and then rafted through the pass or hauled by the CCC logging trucks.

Hoypus Point has many acres of old growth forest awaiting exploration by hikers. Half of the area is set aside as a Natural Forest Area, where the only development is hiking trails for people.

The south half of Hoypus Hill came into park ownership when the Department of Natural Resources transferred it to State Parks in the early nineties. The southern half is open for horses and bicycles. Lush vegetation growing in numerous wetlands keeps this area like a green cathedral year round.

Trails and Signposts

We now look at trail work of the Camp Rosario enrollees north of the pass.

Right:
Hauling surface material for a foot trail. Location not readily identifiable, but the quality of work is evident, with a raised bed, crowned shape, and drainage off the sides in the foreground.

Trails and Signposts

Trails and Signposts

Trails and Signposts

Above:
Trail construction, location undetermined.

Below:
More handwork, on the Lighthouse Point Trail.

253

Trails and Signposts

Above
The writing on the original print says "a mountain trail at the seashore." Truly, the trail from Rosario to Reservation Bay hugs the cliff edge. The drop-off on the water side of the trail is as steep as it looks, as vertical as it looks, and as far as it looks. Today, a railing stands between the trail and the cliff at this area. In the background, the new development area at Reservation Bay looks like an inviting — and safer — place to be.

Photograph from the Washington State Digital Archives.

Below:
A dry rock wall on the Rosario—Reservation Bay trail. The slope here was very unstable. "Dry rock" means no mortar is used to hold the rocks together.

Trails and Signposts

Left:
A typical sign post, this one on the trail to Lighthouse Point. The left sign points to Reservation Bay, the right signs point to Light House Pt. and Canoe Pass Lower, and in the background to an unknown location at top, then Pass Lake and Canoe Pass Upper, presumably the trail that leads eastward from this junction toward the bridge.

Below:
Pick axe and rake to build more trail on Lighthouse Point. Note three men in the background along with the two in the foreground.

Following page:
A completed trail in the Lighthouse Point area.

Trails and Signposts

Trails and Signposts

Above:
A well-made bridge on the Rosario—Reservation Bay trail, spanning a drainage ravine.

Following page:
The state archives include this picture by renowned photographer Asahel Curtis. It illustrates his usual attention to perfection in composition, lighting, and detail. The two hikers are resting on the edge of the trail that leads to Lighthouse Point from Reservation Bay.

View looking north towards the bay, showing the beach line.

In the distance, the kitchen shelter can be seen just above the beach before the beach gets obscured by the needles of the tree at the left side foreground.

Photograph from the Washington State Digital Archives.

Trails and Signposts

Trails and Signposts

Above:
Approaching Park Entrance sign for westbound Highway 20, near the west end of Pass Lake. At this time, most of the land around Pass Lake was in private ownership, so the park entrance did not begin until just west of here.

Below:
The park's official entrance at the west end of Pass Lake had this welcoming sign. The left signs point across the bridge to Deception Pass, Cranberry Lake, and North Beach. The right sign points back east to Anacortes via Sharp Corner. Partially hidden in the back is a sign that says Reservation Bay. A sign for Rosario cannot be seen, if it existed at all. From the shadows it appears to not be here. Pass Creek, the outlet of Pass Lake, is in the drainage behind the sign.

Both photographs from the Washington State Digital Archives.

Trails and Signposts

Above:
The same sign as the one on the previous page, with Pass Lake in the background to the east of the sign, and the new Highway 20 partially visible hugging the shoreline on the right side of the picture.

Right:
A worker building trail on "the rugged sides of Goose Rock," the picture states.

TABLES

Whereas buildings and roads have to be engineered to follow precise architectural mandates, tables can be built however the builder feels, led by creativity and ingenuity.

That appears to be the standard when it came to picnic tables at Deception Pass State Park; that is, there were no standards, other than to take native materials and make a structure that theoretically could be used by someone to enjoy a meal.

Some of the tables pictured here are works of exquisite craftsmanship. Some are works of whimsy that don't appear to have even the remotest hope of being used, certainly not for any length of time.

Many of them display what Albert Good called "an agreeable disregard for true planes and straight edges."

Most of the tables are of massive size and scale, with table tops built from solid slabs of tree that are at least four or five inches thick, and with dimensions of four feet wide by eight feet long or more. Where they found trees suitable to create table tops of that size can only be imagined, but we know they came from the park. The forests here offer superlative, unexcelled opportunities to develop such massively scaled tables that we can rest assured that a handful of picnicking dads will not be able to move them a few feet further to get a better view.

These are one-of-a-kind creations, built out of the materials on hand by the bare hands of CCC members. Their true uniqueness must have been a marvel for those park visitors who had the privilege of discovering these tables in the picnic areas at Deception Pass.

These visitors may not have been quite as appreciative when they discovered how the unmilled, hand-hewn tops and edges were not friendly to silk stockings or other light clothing.

That we have now accepted the milled and manufactured tables, with metal legs, standard sized lumber, and machined bolts to hold them together shows how far our culture has changed, and how our expectations of a park's facilities have accepted the practical limits of mass production and economy over the previous norm of resource-intensive and time-consuming craftsmanship.

Tables

Above:
Hewing out table tops. The original CCC picnic tables were hand built, on-site, out of native materials. What kind of trees were felled to allow building table tops like these?

Below:
Hauling the benches and table tops to their final destination.

Tables

Tables

Previous page and this page: Examples of the hand-built tables and benches installed throughout Deception Pass by the CCC.

The craftsmanship is superb. The table in the middle shows some of the details of the construction. Notes on the original picture mention that no nails were used to join the wood, just dowels.

Tools of the trade still lie against or on top of the bench in the photo at the top.

Tables

Both of the tables on this page appear to be in the same area, with the same shelter in the background

Tables

Above:
Three hand-crafted tables just to the south of the East Cranberry Lake shelter, looking out over Cranberry Lake. The sign in the background points to Cranberry Lake Road, West Beach, and North Beach.

Right:
Another table of unknown location, but obviously built with quality workmanship.

Tables

A table at Little North Beach, with stumps holding up the table top and perhaps some of the legs as well! Deception Island in the distance. Gun Point in the background has no trees on it at this time. This same table may be the same table as the one pictured below, as seen from the other side of the table.

Tables

Three more tables. The table at the bottom appears to be at North Beach.

The table on the left uses rocks to hold up the table top and benches!

Tables

Above:
The sign and bench combination seen earlier in the "Trails and Signposts" chapter, here seen being put to good use by an enrollee, unless he is supposed to be working.

Below:
Yet another combination of wooden planks for the table and benches, with rocks and the trunk of a tree holding them up. Perhaps this isn't the ideal location for a picnic site, but the creativity is undeniable.

Tables

Above:
A standard design for a table, except for its length, which appears to be about four meters or more. Cranberry Lake is in the background. Photograph from the Washington State Digital Archives.

Below:
With the stockade in the background, this table may have been at the Cornet Bay Camp.

CAMP LIFE

He had a little smile on his face after being issued clothing, and walking down the "shot line." But that night, lying in a strange bed, in a rugged cabin shared with dozens of strangers, and thousands of miles from home and mom, this boy of seventeen or eighteen may have shed a few tears.

Remembering the military men barking orders and scheduling every step he made today and knowing it will be like this for the next six months, he knew this great adventure was going to be different from life back home.

It didn't take him long to get into the routine of camp life, however, and he made friends with some of the other boys, away from their homes too for the first time in their young lives.

Hard work and good food molded him into a young man, making a new life for himself.

That first payday was really something. Five dollars was his to spend as he wanted. He spent some of it on candy bars along with toilet paper at the company canteen. He saved some for the ride into town on Saturday night in the same truck he had ridden to work in each day, only now it was all cleaned up with board seats in the back for the boys where there had been tools and lumber.

Coming back to camp was a different ride, half asleep, trying not to lie on the next fella's shoulder, or to keep the other guy off of his.

Yes, he worked forty hours a week. But there was ample time for learning and camp work, for recreation and exploration and visiting the nearby communities of Oak Harbor and Anacortes, for making friends and making memories.

During the day they worked for the park. Camp life became their life while they lived and breathed as CCC boys. Enrollees rose from their barracks at 0600 and reported to physical training at 0630. After breakfast and formation, they spent the next eight hours at work sites around the park, returning to camp at 1600.

Back in camp they were supervised by the Department of War. They ate from army dishes, slept under army blankets, turned out for full dress inspections, and listened to "taps" at the end of each day.

Evenings and weekends were set aside for leisure, unless there was unfinished labor to be done. In their free time enrollees played sports, studied in the camp library, and even published a bi-monthly newspaper. Life was good in the CCC. As the next few pages demonstrate, they worked hard in the park, and they played hard in camp, enjoying life, gaining an education, exploring new opportunities, and making lifelong friendships.

Mel Kahn, an enrollee in a different corner of Washington State, said "I think, basically, you learned to stand on your own two feet. It was the greatest time of my life."

Camp Life

Safety should always be of the highest importance for any work team, and so it was for the CCC. The next few photos show some of the training examples they used, and some of the problems they encountered.

Above:
A trained and knowledgeable woodsman teaches new enrollees about the skills of felling a tree of large size. This looks like a Western red cedar about to become lumber for some park project.

Below:
The techniques have changed drastically over the years, but the message is the same: first aid is a valuable skill for everyone to have. Here they practice artificial respiration in the manner of the thirties: compressions on the back to stimulate breathing.

Camp Life

Safety training had to cover a variety of tasks and tools. The men of the CCC worked at a host of potentially dangerous jobs. In an era before OSHA and WISHA, there were few protections available to the common worker except to be as careful — and as smart — as possible.

Here, an unsafe (left) and safe (below) way to split a piece of wood. Either method has risk, but the danger of using the method on the left is obvious.

Camp Life

Dangerous (above) and safer (right) methods of carrying a crosscut saw with others around. Those teeth are sharp, and on uneven ground, anything can happen without warning.

Camp Life

Unsafe (left) and safe (below) way to handle a peavey on a slope with a log. On the left, the tooth of the peavey will come out if the log begins to roll, leaving the tool as an unhelpful impediment instead of as a force for good.

Below, the tooth of the peavey digs into the log to allow the tool to stop any rolling motion.

Camp Life

Above:
Vehicles or other motorized equipment can always be a source of accidents. The X marks the spot where a bulldozer ran into trouble on a slippery road, perhaps on the Reservation Bay roadway. The skid marks are still visible.

Below:
The photo print says simply "Final resting place." Presumably, it was final only for a short amount of time until it could be removed and repaired, as they could not afford to leave equipment like this off in the brush. What happened to the operator is unknown.

The work of the CCC was often hazardous, as they operated heavy equipment, cut down old growth trees, blasted through solid rock, and slung sharp tools throughout the course of their work day with little or no safety equipment.

Camp Life

Above:
With a limited amount of power equipment but an abundance of manpower, sometimes the easiest way to get a job done is to get everyone pulling in the same direction.

Here they are lined up in two lines to pull a camp toilet up the hill at Cornet Bay. Although the backstory is lost to antiquity, the possibilities are open for the imagination.

Camp Life

Above:
The two camps sometimes engaged in contests against each other. Here they are competing in a single bucking contest, hosted at Cornet Bay against the Rosario camp.

Below:
The two camps now challenging each other to a falling contest, seeing which camp can saw through a similar log in the least amount of time.

Camp Life

Left:
Memorial Day field meet among the camp attendees. The challenge here is to get to the top of the pole and back down again as quickly as possible.

The photo says "10 seconds up & down." This may be the record time achieved, or simply the time achieved by this contestant. Regardless, that is an admirable time for a difficult task, holding on to the climbing rope that is used to shimmy up the pole.

Notice his feet and legs completely free of the pole.

Below:
In the corner of the camp at Cornet Bay, an educator set up a Forestry Museum, used for illustrating the lecture in the forestry school portion of the camp. Cross sections from different species of trees are on display for enrollees to learn about the inhabitants of the Pacific Northwest forests.

Camp Life

Above:
The Rosario 948th Company Baseball team, posing at an unknown location. Cougar Gap may be visible in the background.

Below:
The basketball team from Camp Rosario, with a basketball that says District Champs, 1935. Camp teams usually played against teams from the neighboring community, in this case Anacortes. This team had uniform shirts and even sweatshirts with the number "948" across the front.

Camp Life

Above:
The CCC entered a float in 1935, probably in the Oak Harbor parade. The picture is taken at Cornet Bay as they are on their way to the parade. The sign says US CCC on the left, with a stylized tree. The trail sign says West Point pointing to the right, and beneath that a sign that says North Beach Trail.

Below:
Local members of an unknown tribe put on a demonstration for the camp at Cornet Bay. The people kneeling on the ground carry authentic canoe paddles, and appear to be simulating a voyage on the sea.

Camp Life

Above:
Camp members and visitors sit around a fire at the Cornet Bay amphitheater.

Right:
An enrollee examines a bat. Further details about the photo are unavailable.

"This matter of education — few of you peavies realize how important it is. You all think that you have acquired enough schooling. Nights and weekends are your own. It is shameful to use them in idle pursuits. Take the right step — join one of the classes that interests you most."

— J. Thomashefsky, 1935,
Assistant. Educational Adviser,
Camp Deception Pass

Camp Life

Camp Deception Pass at Cornet Bay published a bi-weekly newsletter, as did most of the camps nationwide. Each edition was eight or ten pages, with editorial comments, company information, safety reminders, encouraging words, jokes, poetry, cartoons, sports news, world news, and anything else that could be typed and published in the camp office.

One article, written by an Edward Gulden, typed out a description of life in a camp.

It's astonishing how fast a fellow gets into the swing of the "Army" life, the spirit of the Camp.

You're a rookie only a short time, for it is easy to cultivate friends. You learn the sayings of the camp, "hand-shaking", "lobby-gowing", "stooge", and etc.; you learn the tricks that are played "short-sheeting" for instance and the well known "snipe hunt".

Days pass pleasantly, too swiftly. At times nostalgia sets in but amiable surrounds soon disperse melancholy hearth-stone pangs.

At nights there are classes to attend, a well stocked library to browse in, and ping-pong tables in the recreation hall. Motion pictures are shown once a week in the mess hall, trucks are run to town every weekend for recreational purposes.

If one prefers fishing, hiking, rowing and the likes instead, it's right in his own backyard. Yes sir, the CCC's are a fine organization and a credit to the present administration.

Camp Life

Left:
Dodging the waves at West Point, a favorite Sunday walk for the camp members as it remains for park visitors today. Lighthouse Point is in the background across the water.

Below:
Some of the crew sitting around one the tables they had built, enjoying a watermelon together.

Photos courtesy of John Tursi.

Camp Life

The interior of one of the bunkhouses, showing two of the bunks. Notice the army-discipline in the appearance of the shoes under the bed, the blankets on the bed, and the cleanliness throughout.

The wood stove on the left was the only source of heat.

"They took us down to the washroom area where they had new bales of straw. We had to fill these mattress covers with the straw. Quite a joke around camp that after you filled the mattress up you couldn't get any sleep for the first couple of nights because you'd lay there and listen to the straw tick."

—Elbert Cranfill, enrollee

Camp Life

Above:

An intimate look at the desk of a supervisor at the camp at Cornet Bay. The ensuing decades may have changed the technology seen on a typical office desk, but the framework remains startlingly similar: chair, desk, lamp, family photos, monthly calendar, a word processor, files, writing tools, papers tacked to the wall, and a clock hung above the window in this corner office.

This office was at Rosario Camp. The typewriter is an LC Smith and Brothers. The calendar says October 1934. An ashtray sits in the middle of the desk. Knob and tube wiring, nailed to the window frame, runs to the light and clock and elsewhere. What appears to be a schedule is on the wall to the right. The window is open in October, so it must have been a warm and sunny day. The time is two minutes before one o'clock.

Camp Life

Above:
Decorations in the mess hall in preparation for a Christmas celebration.

Below:
A festive gathering in the mess hall ready for campers to feast.

Camp Life

Above:
What may be the same day as the previous photo, enlarged and looking in towards the kitchen to see the size of the crew that it takes to provide a meal three times a day at the camp.

"We came from very poverty-ridden circumstances. For many days maybe a little bowl of soup a day would be it. We just didn't eat. But the food out here was just fantastic. To wake up and go into all the hot cakes you could eat and all the butter you wanted and milk and eggs."

—John Tursi

Camp Life

Above:
Inside the Mess Hall, with several servers and cooks posed at their work places. Green boughs are attached to the windows and are gracing some of the tables.

Many of the CCC enrollees didn't care so much about getting money, which was mostly sent back home, as they did about getting three full meals a day, something many of them had never experienced before. The average enrollee gained over 11 pounds during their short stay at the camp.

Camp Life

Above:
A load of young men ready to go home from Cornet Bay. How their lives have changed in the past six months is a story to be repeated dozens of times when they get back home.

Right:
The writing at the bottom says:

"To Gordon
It was certainly good to
have you here
S E Anderson."

The camp roster March 1934 shows S. E. Anderson as the 2nd Lieutenant Eng. Res., second in command for the camp under G. R. Bostain. A note in the margin of our copy of the roster points to Anderson's name and says "My Buddy."

"I watched these kids that I was with grow physically, emotionally, and socially. but I didn't realize it was happening to me until I compared myself with the guys that hadn't gone."

—Herb Valentine, Enrollee

PARK SCENERY

"...cold and wild the surf,
rushing in to overwhelm
the beach, the wind, stinging
my cheeks,
enveloping me
in total freedom."
— Scott Holman

Scenery is such a generic word that it can be almost banal in its use. When applied to this park, however, the word rises to an entirely different level of meaning.

Understandably, the National Park Service photographer did not confine his work to documenting the projects of the CCC. He also explored some of the many scenic and photogenic landscapes located throughout Deception Pass.

The following section highlights some of these extra photographs as a tribute to the beauty of Deception Pass State Park, and as a photographic record of what the park used to look like before additional development after the CCC, and future park managers, changed the landscape forever.

Forever is a strong word, and not at all accurate, as more changes will occur in future generations. Some of these changes will hopefully restore some of the natural beauty and cultural sacredness of the sites that have been damaged.

But the inertia of current use is hard to overcome. The popularity of the development at West Beach, for example, will counterbalance any interest in restoring the natural dune beach that was here for thousands of years. The necessity of high tension power lines across Goose Rock outweighs any aesthetic desire to have a clear skyline and views of the pass.

On the other hand, because of the CCC, many other destructive developments have been avoided. Efforts to expand parking in places such as Rosario and Bowman Bay are stopped because of the landscape plan of the CCC to limit the amount of vehicles in these areas, which also limits the impact of large numbers of people on sensitive resources. It also preserves the experience of being on top of Rosario Head, for example, with a reasonable expectation of solitude, shared only with a handful of others, the soaring of an eagle overhead, and the passage of a seal or dolphin in the waters below.

We are not born into this land, we are born out of it, like a wave from the sea.

The beauty of the Deception Pass area overwhelms the first-time visitor here. It becomes ingrained into anyone who spends time here, and in turn becomes the heart song of those who allow themselves to be filled with its glory.

Man is not himself only...He is all that he sees; all that flows to him from a thousand sources...He is the land, the lift of its mountain lines, the reach of its valleys."
— Mary Austin

Park Scenery

Above:
Taken from the trail between Rosario and Reservation Bay. Reservation Head and West Point are in the background.

Next page:
This photo appears to be taken closer to Rosario than the picture on the left, with Deception Island in the distance.

Scenery

Park Scenery

Park Scenery

Previous page:
As seen from Sayres Head north of Rosario Beach, Rosario Head is connected to Rosario Beach by a tombolo, a word meaning a spit of land connecting a land mass to what would otherwise be an island. Notice the old truck parked on the tombolo, and what appear to be structures of some kind on the grassy land to the left.

Above:
The master plan for Deception Pass State Park called for the entire West Beach area to be left intact as a natural beach and forest environment. The feeling of this beach is far different than what one experiences standing in the same location today. This view of West Beach is from the current location of the Sand Dune Interpretive Trail, south of the concession stand, looking northward.

Park Scenery

Above:
Taken from what is now the middle of the West Beach parking area, this view looking northwesterly towards Deception Island shows a thick concentration of logs and woody debris on the shoreline of West Beach.

The ferocity of the storm and the abundance of driftwood indicate the this may be a winter or springtime picture.

Following page:
West Beach, as seen from what is now the southern end of the parking lot. Fifteen years later this scene will be replaced with the Cranberry Lake road coming from the right and a two-hundred car parking lot.

Park Scenery

Park Scenery

Above:
Looking north from the southern boundary in the dunes area at West Beach. Driftwood litters the foreshore dunes, an indicator of a healthy, thriving beach environment.

Below:
Cranberry Lake is immediately adjacent to West Beach, separated only by the dunes.

Park Scenery

Above:
A bench sits beside a trail along the north shore of Cranberry Lake. A roadway now takes the place of this trail. The large rock face on the right side of the picture is now a popular fishing hole.

Below:
The view from what was then the new parking lot at the south end of the also-new Deception Pass Bridge. Today this view is blocked from the parking lot by a new growth of Douglas fir trees on the slope near the parking area. Deception Island sits off the pass in the distance, with Lopez Island in the far distance beyond. Lighthouse Point is on the right side of the picture.

Park Scenery

Left:
A view west from the top of Goose Rock, with Deception Island in the distance.

Below:
Another view from the top of Goose Rock, showing a power line on the shoulder of the hill, and Deception Island to the west.

On the right side of the picture, left to right, we can see Lighthouse Point, Northwest Island just peaking out beyond a hill, and the bluff of Sayres Head just north of Rosario. Lopez Island is in the far distance in the left center.

Park Scenery

Above:
The top of Goose Rock had few trees in the thirties, and an abundance of wildflowers growing on what is called a "bald," the shallow soil carpeting the bedrock of the hill. Trees struggle to grow in this shallow soil, but wildflowers and native grasses are well adapted to the difficult conditions. They are sensitive to heavy foot traffic, however, and if trampled frequently will be replaced by common weed species.

Below:
The view northeast from the top of Goose Rock, with Strawberry Island in the near distance and Mount Erie rising in the far distance beyond.

Park Scenery

From the eastern slope of Goose Rock, looking eastward, over Ben Ure Island to Hoypus Point beyond, with Yokeko Point on the far left side.

The house on the rock shoulder of Ben Ure Island is still occupied today. The shed barely visible on the front right corner of the island was removed just a few years ago after it collapsed.

The margin of the original print of this photo labels the island as "Barnes Island," an earlier name for this island. The name Ben Ure commemorates a colorful and notorious former resident of the island from the nineteenth century.

Park Scenery

Above:
A view of North Beach, taken from the trail leading from the bridge down to the beach. A sailboat appears to be anchored or at rest off North Beach; Gun Point is in the foreground. Little North Beach is at the very bottom of the picture. The view from here has changed very little.

Photograph from the Washington State Digital Archives.

Following page:
A calm and clear day at North Beach, taken not far from West Point. Deception Island basks in the sun offshore.

Park Scenery

Park Scenery

From Deception Island looking east toward Deception Pass, the view as Captain Vancouver would have seen it. Pass Island is in the left center of the picture. Canoe Pass is hidden by the shores of Lighthouse Point on the left.

Park Scenery

Two more views of Deception Pass before the bridge was built.

Above:
From the eastern shore of Deception Island looking east to the pass, similar to the view on the previous page.

Below:
From Hoypus Point looking westward towards the pass. Strawberry Island is in the foreground, Pass Island is partially hidden behind. The main pass is between Pass Island and Goose Rock on the left side of the picture.

Park Scenery

A closer view of Deception Pass, taken from the southern end of Lighthouse Point, looking eastward into the throat of the Pass. Canoe Pass can be seen on the left, Deception Pass on the right, with Pass Island in the middle.

Park Scenery

Standing on Lottie Point, the view of Deception Pass is dramatic. Pass Island is on the left, Goose Rock on the right. The bridge would soon connect these two points of land and Fidalgo Island to the north.

Park Scenery

The rocky outcrop in the foreground is surrounded by water at high tide, and difficult to climb even at low tide. Someone built a very attractive footbridge sometime before this photograph was taken.

The foot bridge no longer exists.

It appears that little work has yet been done on the future Deception Pass Bridge beyond.

Park Scenery

This photograph is taken from near where the bridge stood in the picture on the previous page, or perhaps it may have even been taken from that bridge, looking toward the pass.

Someone has drawn a line on this photograph indicating very closely where the new bridge will be built to give viewers an idea of what to expect.

Park Scenery

Two views of Canoe Pass, this page and the next, both taken from Lottie Point, both looking eastward between Bowman Hill and Pass Island.

Park Scenery

Park Scenery

Compare this picture with the previous pictures to see some subtle differences in the landscape, along with the obvious change of the new Canoe Pass span of the Deception Pass Bridge under construction.

Strawberry Island and Hoypus Hill can be seen in the distance beyond Canoe Pass.

Park Scenery

The bridge completed and ready for use. Photo taken from the northwest corner of the parking lot south of the bridge, before new trees grew on the fresh soil created by the construction project. The trail in the foreground goes to North Beach.

Photograph from the Washington State Digital Archives.

EPILOGUE

Regardless of its value for building parks and training men, the Civilian Conservation Corps was generally seen as a relief agency. With rising employment rates in the early forties and dwindling enrollment in the Corps, the program could no longer be justified. So with the onset of World War II, the CCC was disbanded.

Though the last enrollees left in 1942, their presence will long be felt at Deception Pass. In the bleakest of times the Corps gave these young men a chance, and in return they built a legacy. Their work at the park is a testament to ingenuity, teamwork, and the restorative power of nature. They were not merely building structures, but also building stewardship – preserving and protecting this special place so that future generations might enjoy their labor as well.

Three million young men were enrolled in the program nationwide. An estimated twelve to fifteen million family members were able to get through the Great Depression and back on their feet again because of the CCC, a tremendous bargain for an investment in our people and our resources.

As the enrollees of the CCC grew older, and eventually retired from their careers, they recognized that their experiences in the CCC composed a grand story, a story that would fade with time unless someone captured it soon.

In 1978, some alumni from the Seattle area created an officially recognized chapter to meet regularly and seek ways they could preserve the story of the CCC. They were the fifth chapter in the nation to so organize, and thus became Chapter 5 of the National Association of CCC Alumni. In a couple of years their membership rolls listed 310 participants.

A few years later, alumni in the Everett area also formed a chapter, designated Chapter 78, and led by former CCC enrollee Vic Olsen.

Vic had worked for the CCC at Camp Easton, near Cle Elum, and then Camp Louella near Sequim. Like many of the CCC enrollees, Vic was asked to use dynamite to blast rock for various projects. Vic was critically injured at one point, and received an honorable discharge.

> *"'The end of the CCC.' Those words fill us with a bit of sadness. For over nine years now this organization of ours has given hope and inspiration to thousands of young men throughout our nation. Perhaps no single agency in all history has so profoundly influenced a nation in so short a span. The imprint it has made on the life of our nation will live forever."*
>
> —Leonard C. Gaskill, CCC District Adjutant

After retirement, he and his wife Mae asked other alumni living near them to share memorabilia they may have with the hope of starting a viewable collection. Members brought in so many pictures and mementos that they knew they should get them displayed in a museum somewhere.

After years of searching, they met with Washington State Parks director Jan Tveten, and the head of State Parks Interpretive Services,

Dick Clifton, who offered the bathhouse at Bowman Bay as a possible interpretive center site. The alumni were delighted.

It took more than three years of group work parties to renovate the building, which had been unused since World War II. More than 50 alumni took part on various weekends, gathering appropriate materials, cleaning the building inside and out, and preparing it for the exhibits being constructed by State Parks staff.

The exhibits tell the story of the CCC throughout the state of Washington, with memorabilia, photos, diaries, life size displays, and personal stories shared by members of Chapter 78 and others. Alumni, park staff, and a crowd of visitors dedicated the center on July 16, 1988.

Vic and Mae stayed at the Bowman Bay campground as campground hosts for many years, and volunteered their time at the interpretive center to tell stories of the CCC to those who were interested. Some months brought over 3,000 visitors through the museum.

Chapter 5 challenged their members at the 70th anniversary of the CCC in 2003 to see if they could raise the funds for a specially designed life-sized statue of a CCC worker. Chapters around the country were attempting to display one statue in each state of the union. With Deception Pass as the iconic home of CCC interpretation for the state of Washington, Chapter 5 approached State Parks about the possibility of adding the statue at Deception Pass.

We agreed in principle that Bowman Bay would be an ideal location. And we knew that raising the funds would not be easy. However, we did not realize the persistence and effectiveness of the alumni. Bob Robeson, Walter Bailey, John Hamilton, Jiggs Hudson, Albert Roundtree, and alumni spouse Berniece Phelps, along with many others of Chapter 5, came through. They raised enough money to have the statue built. State Parks and a variety of charitable sources found enough money to have the statue shipped to the park. Park maintenance staff Mark Lunz, Marvin Wold, and Dan Dillard built a base to support the statue, using CCC-inspired methods for the rockwork.

On September 18, 2004, the statue was unveiled to a crowd of over 200 gathered at Bowman Bay, commemorating the 28th statue to be installed in the United States, and the only one for the state of Washington.

The original CCC Interpretive Center organizers, shown here posing in 1988 at the first work party for the new center.
Front row: Walt Bailey, Jiggs Hudson, and Floyd Olson.
Back row: Del Sells, Taffy Sells, Verla Bailey, Russ Bean, Mae Olsen, Irene Olson, and Vic Olsen.

In a speech held in the upper CCC shelter at Bowman Bay, State Parks Director Rex Derr congratulated the CCC alumni for their stewardship in building parks and for their dedication in preserving and sharing the story of the CCC.

In March of 2008, on the 75th anniversary of the CCC, Chapter 5, Chapter 78, and other CCC alumni organized bus trips to come to Cornet Bay for a chance to get together and celebrate the 75th anniversary of the creation of the

CCC. Park interpreter Adam Lorio recorded oral histories of several of the alumni as they shared their memories. Everyone gathered in the dining hall that stood where the original dining hall stood 75 years earlier. At the end of congratulatory speeches, attendees enjoyed a large 75th birthday cake.

That year, the average age of the remaining CCC alumni was now over eighty-five. Chapter membership numbers were declining rapidly. In 2010, Chapter 5 officially dissolved their association after 32 years of service, inviting park staff to say goodbye with them, and giving the remaining funds in their association to the Deception Pass Park Foundation for interpretive efforts.

The statue of a CCC worker installed on a stone base near the CCC Interpretive Center at Bowman Bay.

In that same year, The Deception Pass Park Foundation sponsored an interpretive sign to tell the story of a young man who came from the East Coast to Cornet Bay back in the early years of the CCC, to start a new life as an enrollee. That young man spent two years at Cornet Bay, from 1934 to 1936, building the highway to the bridge, building the underpass beneath, and working throughout the south side of the park.

The interpretive sign, installed at the west end of the underpass, illustrates the building of the underpass, and honors the work that the young man accomplished back then and continues to offer today. That under-aged enrollee, John Tursi, went on to serve his country in World War II, become a successful manager at the Shell refinery, and also become a beloved CCC alumni, cherished for his generosity in supporting the virtues of the CCC. He helped people and funded the preservation of parks and our natural resources.

Mr. Tursi has contributed grandly with his stories, his time, and his money for so many projects in the area. His kindness and care for this land and its people will never be forgotten. The interpretive sign is one way we wanted others to recognize how Mr. Tursi has benefited us all.

Together, the people of the CCC changed the course of the nation. They built parks, preserved farmland and forests, protected our resources, and served their country well. At the same time, they grew in character, and created a backbone of stable families that returned our nation to economic strength.

The generation of the CCC has almost come to its end. The inexorable march of time inevitably takes its toll. It is with great sadness that we say goodbye to these friends who have inspired us for so many years, and whose legacy will continue to inspire us.

The work they accomplished at Deception Pass stands as their tribute, their honor, and their gift to an enduring future.

Right:
With the underpass in the background, John Tursi stands beside the interpretive sign that honors his story and the work of the CCC at Deception Pass State Park.

Below:
Members of the local Civilian Conservation Corps alumni chapters gather at the CCC Interpretive Center at Bowman Bay during a reunion picnic held there around 2007.

SINCE THE CCC

So what has changed since these structures and park features were built so many years ago?

Deception Pass State Park became a popular destination with these new projects, a developed park with facilities to meet the needs of visitors.

And people came in droves. By the early seventies, the park was seeing well over a million visitors a year. By the eighties, this had climbed to two, three, four, even five million visitors in busy years, higher numbers than even most national parks around the country.

Park development increased to keep pace with the growing demand. The small campgrounds of the CCC days were expanded and then expanded further to eventually have the highest number of campsites of any state park in Washington. Roadways were pushed to West Beach. Capital projects built boat launches at Cornet Bay and Bowman Bay. The Department of Fisheries built a hatchery and pier at Bowman Bay as well, south of the CCC facilities there, drastically changing the scenery of the bay. When the hatchery was discontinued in the early seventies, the dock and brick residence were added to the list of park features as well.

Unfortunately, some of the Corps-built structures or park features have been altered beyond recognition, or removed entirely. The bathhouse at East Cranberry Lake was demolished decades ago. The reason for its removal is not known at this time. A contractor was hired in about 1970 to "remove and level the remaining foundation" of the bathhouse. Why such a massive structure would have fallen into disrepair in just three decades is a mystery.

A handful of CCC features are no longer necessary as designed, such as a second restroom at East Cranberry Lake, or the bathhouse at Reservation Bay. These have been adapted to serve new purposes. The restroom, for example, now houses a backup generator to power nearly all of the park's sewer treatment needs. The Reservation Bay bathhouse is now the CCC Interpretive Center. The restroom built by Corps members at Rosario has been remodeled on the inside to be a field classroom for beach education programs. All of these buildings look the same externally, but have new life inside.

Most of the temporary Cornet Bay camp structures were taken down when the camp ended, as intended, leaving behind the camp landscape of a central playfield, and three permanent structures: the amphitheater fireplace, an incinerator, and a small picnic shelter. A vehicle accident knocked down the picnic shelter in 2008, but park staff saved the pieces, allowing a 2013 historical preservation class to have an opportunity to rebuild the shelter with authentic methods and materials while teaching new historians and maintenance staff about the skills of the CCC.

The Rosario camp was situated on what is now private property. The camp was decommissioned when it ended, and virtually no immediately recognizable trace now remains.

The distinctive and much loved guardrails along Highway 20 were built for a time when cars were smaller, lighter, and slower. Today's vehicles using Highway 20 include dump trucks with trailers, 18-wheelers, RVs, and a plethora of commuter traffic, up to 20,000 vehicles a day all told.

The design of the original CCC railings could no longer stop a vehicle from going over the edge.

The Washington State Department of Transportation built new railings to replace critical areas of the historical guardrail. Washington

State Parks encouraged the design of these railings to reflect the legacy of the CCC while still being engineered to handle modern traffic needs.

The new railing system, installed in 2005, looks fairly similar to what the CCC built, but it can withstand a direct impact by a sizeable truck moving at a fairly high speed. Indeed, in 2013 a northbound dump truck towing a trailer struck a section of the railing north of the bridge nearly head on. The truck bounced off, eventually careening over and through a section of the original CCC rails further down the highway, stopped from going over the cliff only by a sizeable tree at the edge.

Other alterations to the CCC legacy are more subtle, happening over time, sometimes accidentally, sometimes through neglect or lack of funding or staff time to address all the maintenance needs of these aging structures or to address them appropriately.

Historic trails get altered by erosion or other earth movement. Fence lines get changed to meet new trail safety requirements. Roofs get replaced with different sized shakes or support beams to save money and time, or because there aren't enough large cedar trees to create shakes of the same size the CCC had used. Foundations need to be replaced after decades of standing on wet soil. Trees fall through roofs, cars bump buildings, wood rots, budgets get tight, usage changes.

Changes to the landscapes can be even more innocuous. The CCC created specific spaces with purposeful intent. For example, they planted trees next to some of the shelters to frame the buildings, to give them a natural backdrop and scalable reference point. However, trees grow and become too large, too old, or diseased. Many of the original landscape trees at Bowman Bay and East Cranberry Lake have had to be removed, changing the design of the area.

The original National Park Service plans for the viewpoints at the bridge included sweeping vistas that took advantage of the barren cliff faces. Today, trees have become established on the slopes due to the original rock construction debris having been dumped down the hillside. The debris fields hold water and are now supporting tree roots. These trees have become substantial over the past 75 years, and block many of the views that the CCC expected visitors to enjoy when they parked in the turnouts.

Although park management does not usually advocate for cutting trees, this is one situation where selective thinning will actually restore the safety of the turnouts by maintaining the historical CCC viewpoints as they were intended, instead of forcing people to try to get close to the cliff edge to get a better picture.

A classic restroom building constructed by the CCC resides at East Cranberry Lake in a location no longer used by many people. The building was adapted to house a generator that is the backup power for the park sewer system — a mundane use, certainly, but also necessary, and accommodated without having to alter the appearances of the outside.

Ongoing park development can alter a landscape as well, such as putting a garbage dumpster next to a shelter, or creating a park entrance next to a picnic and swimming beach, or plowing an entirely new road down to a previously untouched beach area, or building a new restroom near a historical kitchen shelter. All of these changes have happened here in the past.

The once-popular swimming beach at East Cranberry has faded with time due to a drastic alteration to the park landscape, counter to the park's original plans. A park manager wanted visitors to have easier access to West Beach, so he cut and plowed a road to the beach.

West Beach itself was eventually paved over to become a 220 car parking lot, with a concession stand on the spit of beach between Cranberry Lake and the saltwater. With this change, the attention and interest of visitors shifted from the east side of the lake to the west. The new swim beach at the west end of the lake has taken attention away from East Cranberry, so that the original swim beach structure on the east side of the lake has become overgrown and in disrepair.

Overall, however, the feel of the CCC work still remains, the expectation of interacting with a natural environment, of being a part of the environment. Deception Pass still offers that rustic recreational experience for all.

There are twenty-four original CCC buildings still standing at Deception Pass. In addition there are a handful of distinctive CCC features, such as the guardrails along Highway 20, the only ones of their kind left in the state; the amphitheater fireplace and the incinerator at Cornet Bay; the beach at East Cranberry, the tunnel under Highway 20 near North Beach; the rock gateway at Rosario; and the miles of highway, roadway, and trails that the crews developed throughout the park.

The volume of CCC structures and facilities at Deception Pass State Park sets it apart from all other parks in Washington. No other state park has the abundance and quality of CCC landscapes with intact buildings still in place and even in use.

Washington State Parks chose Deception Pass to house the interpretive center that focuses on the story of the CCC in Washington State. Opened in 1988, the center explains the background of the Depression era, illustrates the history of the creation of the CCC, and then with quotes and examples highlights the stories of the CCC workers themselves to keep alive this historical milestone in the history of our parks and nation.

Artifacts, many first collected by the Olsens and their alumni friends, are the real tools, clothes, certificates, footwear, blankets, cooking pots and aprons from the CCC camps. Liberally scattered throughout the exhibits are the words of the enrollees themselves, sharing forever their impressions of what it meant to come of age in the service of building parks.

The interior of the CCC Interpretive Center at Bowman Bay has lively exhibits and memorable quotes.

Current park management has sought to continue the design concepts and values of the CCC in new structures so that the visual landscape will remain unified and consistent. For example, the new park office on Highway 20, the welcome stations at the Cranberry Lake park entrance, three new restrooms in the Cranberry Lake campground, the new restroom and shelter at the Cornet Bay boat launch area, the West Beach shelter and concession building, the restroom at Bowman Bay campground, and the new restroom at Rosario all embrace a standard appearance consisting of a rock base with an upper wall of log or board and batten.

Seeing like-minded structures that make the use of native materials and blend with natural settings throughout the park helps keep the spirit of the CCC design principles alive in the park. This rustic and natural theme identifies park structures as part of the park core, honoring the legacy of the visionary program that first developed this special place.

That honor includes maintaining the existing structures as closely as possible to the original design. Lacking an abundance of enrollees such as the CCC enjoyed, and lacking a budget to dedicate to these facilities, we face an ongoing challenge to keep these arguably temporary buildings in usable condition.

The generosity of time and the skill sets of volunteers and occasional contracted experts help makes this happen. Throughout the past decade, many restorative projects have brought back some of the integrity of the CCC landscape and structures.

In 2002, park staff from throughout the northwest region of the state rebuilt much of the main kitchen shelter at East Cranberry Lake, using original methods and tools that the CCC used to gain a deeper understanding of the techniques and skills that went into the creation of these structures.

In recent years, several members of the Pacific Northwest Trail Association found local cedar wood, split it into authentically sized shakes, and re-roofed the kitchen shelter at North Beach, assisted by park staff.

The rockwork and metal parts in several of the stoves of the shelters degraded over the decades to the point that many of them were unusable. In 2010 and 2011 Ted Lagreid, the son and grandson of former CCC local experienced men, gave liberally of his finances to hire a local stone mason, Bruce Aalmo of Island Masonry, to rebuild two of these stoves to CCC standards with modern applications. These two shelters, one at East Cranberry Lake and one at Little North Beach, have stoves that will endure well into this century

Also in 2010 and 2011, volunteers from HDR Engineering in Seattle took on the task of rebuilding the two little shelters at East Cranberry Lake. Led by Lex Palmer and Martha Weiss, coordinated by state park historian Alex McMurry, and guided by local historical restoration expert Harrison Goodall, they rebuilt and restored these shelters to their original appearances.

Mr. Goodall is a nationally recognized historical restoration specialist. His passion for historical accuracy and preservation is contagious and exceptional. He has devoted hundreds of hours to document our structures and help us make sure projects like this one are successful.

The year 2011 also saw the reconstruction of the Rosario parking area to better reflect the design of the CCC, and brought the grand re-

The renovated interior of the CCC restroom at Rosario Beach. What was a small, outdated and mothballed restroom has become a bright and welcoming place for people to gather and learn about the park history and environment. The exterior has also been restored to its former grandeur.

opening of the mothballed CCC restroom at Rosario's south side. The interior of the restroom is a glorious adaptation of toilet stalls and sinks into a bright and cheery field classroom, using the entire interior space to offer school groups and others a place to gather and learn about the natural and cultural stories that fill this park.

The Deception Pass Park Foundation financed the reconstruction of the rockwork at the amphitheater fireplace and the incinerator at Cornet Bay by another local masonry company, Ward and Johnson, who discounted much of the cost of their work.

This company also repointed the rockwork at the Rosario shelter and the upper Bowman

Bay shelter in 2013, a project also funded by the Deception Pass Park Foundation.

In 2013, dozens of volunteers, organized by the Whidbey Retired Chief Petty Officers Association, stripped the wood of the upper shelter at Bowman Bay down to bare wood, and then treated it with an appropriate preservative to extend the life of the structure. This not only gave the building a longer life, it also restored the original look of natural wood color that the building had when it was built. They also rebuilt the bridge at Bowman Bay on the trail out to Lighthouse Point, another CCC feature often overlooked.

The Deception Pass Park Foundation also sponsored interpretive signage at Cornet Bay. Four sign panels illustrate the story of the CCC camp that developed Cornet Bay, and the stories of the Corps men who worked there, including people like sixteen-year-old John Tursi.

And inside the recreation hall at the Cornet Bay Retreat Center, the Foundation sponsored the reprinting and framing of several of the key historical photographs taken at Cornet Bay, so that campers today and in the future can recognize the work of the CCC in developing these public lands.

And space does not allow us to list the other work that continues throughout the years to keep CCC structures maintained to the degree possible with limited staff and funding. Many of the roofs have been replaced, porches rebuilt, support poles replaced, and landscapes restored to try to preserve this valuable park heritage.

This is all in addition to the ongoing routine cleaning of roofs, replacing broken shingles, scrubbing walls, fixing windows, and other general upkeep of large wooden buildings in a marine shoreline environment in the Pacific Northwest.

Some have said the CCC buildings were not constructed to last this long. Some of the design features, such as wood beams exposed to the elements, suggest this may have been true. The architects and laborers may have considered their structures to be temporary improvements to the park landscape, to be replaced in due time by new facilities.

True or not, the structures are valuable additions and necessary ingredients to the current park landscape. And maintaining what we have is almost always a preferable practice to tearing down part of our heritage for something new.

Throughout the past years of park operations, park staff have done their best to protect and preserve these structures with whatever means they could to keep them functioning and operational. This has required a significant investment of limited park funds and limited staff time.

This is the kind of investment worth our support.

And so today the legacy remains.

It permeates our enjoyment of the park, the vistas we explore, and the values we protect. Preserving the legacy of the Civilian Conservation Corps keeps us connected with the past and sensitive to building a future that furthers our values.

What changes will we see in the future? That is up to us.

Will we continue to honor the legacy handed to us by the previous generations? Will we work with the CCC landscape with respect and understanding, allowing our citizens to enjoy this park as a premier destination of uncommon quality, outstanding for the experience, health, enjoyment, and learning of all people? Will this park continue to inspire, nurture, and restore our visitors? Will recreation also be a re-creation, bringing us back to our roots as we connect with nature, with our culture, with our loved ones, and with each other in community?

And will the park continue to be meaningful in a changing world? Will economic forces drive changes that protect our legacy, or weaken it? Will the work of the CCC be relevant to a new generation that will not have a chance to meet and know the men who did the work?

The answers to these questions are up to us, as we demonstrate with our actions our commitment to this lasting legacy.

FOR FURTHER INFORMATION

Buckley, Esther
Early History of Deception Pass
typed manuscript, 1935

Building Human Happiness: Depression-Era Development of the Washington State Parks, manuscript, undated

Cultural Resources Management Plan for Deception Pass State Park, State of Washington by Marcia Montgomery, Ann Emmons, Delia Hagen, Gail Thompson, and Historical Research Associates, Inc. 2000, 141 pp.

Good, Albert H.
Patterns from the Golden Age of Rustic Design
Roberts Rinehart 2003

Historical Archives Office
Deception Pass State Park
41020 State Route 20
Oak Harbor, WA 98277
360-675-3767

McKinney, Sam
Sailing With Vancouver
TouchWood Editions, 2004, 209 pp.
Maher, Neil M.
Nature's New Deal
Oxford University Press, 2008, 316 pp.

Meany, Edmund S.
Vancouver's Discovery of Puget Sound
Binfords and Mort, 1949, 344 pp.

Neil, Dorothy, and Lee Brainard
By Canoe and Sailing Ship They Came
Spindrift Publishing, 1989, 283 pp.

Pike, Ruth E.
The Washington State Parks Story
Manuscript, ca. 1956

Tursi, John, and Thelma Palmer
Long Journey to the Rose Garden
Fidalgo Bay Publishing, 1989, 198 pp.

Washington State Parks and Recreation Commission
Cherish the Treasure, a History of Washington State Parks 1913 to 1988, 1988, 43 pp. plus appendices

CCC buildings in Deception Pass:
1. Cornet Bay Retreat Center: small shelter *
2. East Cranberry: restroom
3. East Cranberry: restroom converted to diesel engine room, near sewer plant *
4. East Cranberry: pump house, near south boundary
5. East Cranberry: small shelter, south *
6. East Cranberry: kitchen shelter
7. East Cranberry: small shelter, north
8. Old entrance: caretaker's cabin
9. Old entrance: caretaker's garage
10. North Beach: restroom
11. North Beach: Little North Beach shelter
12. North Beach: large shelter
13. North Beach: small shelter *
14. Rosario: kitchen shelter
15. Rosario: pump house *
16. Rosario: restroom
17. Bowman: beach kitchen shelter
18. Bowman: upper kitchen shelter *
19. Bowman: bathhouse/ interpretive center
20. Bowman: small shelter
21. Bowman: caretaker's cabin
22. Bowman: caretaker's garage
23. Bowman: caretaker's barn *
24. Rosario/Bowman: cistern

Starred items indicate buildings or facilities that have no CCC-era photos available for this publication.

Other CCC structures and projects that are still visible:
- North Beach underpass
- Trail from bridge to North Beach and bridge to Goose Rock
- Roadway from East Cranberry to North Beach
- Road (now a trail) from Cornet Bay to North Beach
- Amphitheater fireplace, Cornet Bay Retreat Center
- Incinerator, Cornet Bay Retreat Center *
- Open field, Cornet Bay Retreat Center
- Highway 20 approach to bridge from south, Cornet Bay Road to bridge
- Highway 20 guardrail to bridge from south *
- Rosario parking lot
- Bowman Bay parking areas
- East Cranberry swim beach
- East Cranberry two-level parking area
- Highway 20 approach to bridge from north, Pass Lake to bridge
- Bowman Bay road from Pass Lake to Bowman Bay
- Rosario rock gateway
- Trail from Rosario to Bowman Bay, with a bridge and rockwork
- Trail from Bowman Bay to Lighthouse Point
- Bridge on trail from Bowman Bay to Lighthouse Point

Structures known to be removed:
- East Cranberry Lake bathhouse
- Temporary camp structures at both Cornet Bay and Rosario camps
- Many of the guardrails along Highway 20
- Incinerator between Pass Lake and Bowman Bay.

Modern structures built or modified to reflect CCC heritage:
- East Cranberry Lake entrance station
- East Cranberry Lake little entrance station
- West Beach concession, restroom, and shelter
- Forest Loop Campground restroom, site 60
- Lower Loop Campground restroom, site 90
- Lower Loop Campground restroom, site 97
- Cornet Bay beach area, restroom
- Cornet Bay beach area, picnic shelter
- Park administration building
- Rosario restroom
- Bowman Bay campground restroom
- Newer guardrails, Highway 20
- CCC statue base

ABOUT THE EDITORS

Jack Hartt grew up near the beaches of Puget Sound in the Ballard area of northwest Seattle, in a home that had picture windows that looked toward Whidbey Island and the Olympics.

He first visited Deception Pass State Park as a four-year-old when his family camped at Bowman Bay one weekend. He still remembers that experience, sitting around the campfire eating dinner, smelling the wet but warm canvas tent, and hearing the lapping of waves not far from their campsite. His dad, Al Hartt, took him for a walk to the fish hatchery tanks at the south end of Bowman Bay the next day.

Jack attended Ballard High School and the University of Washington, majoring in park management and interpretation, with his senior thesis being a study of the shoreline management of Washington State Parks.

Summers in college were spent working for the University of Washington as part of a fisheries research team in Alaska; for the United States Forest Service in the Cascades; and as a backcountry ranger for Rocky Mountain National Park in Colorado.

After graduation, he worked at REI in Seattle, as a naturalist at Sun Lakes State Park, and then as a ranger there. His ensuing State Park career has taken him to Camano Island, Cape Disappointment, Ocean City, Olmstead Place, Fort Worden for ten years, Riverside State Park as the park manager for five years, and for the past ten years as manager of Deception Pass State Park, his lasting legacy.

He is a certified personal fitness instructor for Washington State Parks, and was their first master instructor for defensive tactics.

While at Deception Pass he fostered the development of the Deception Pass Park Foundation, the restoration of the Rosario tidepools, the enjoyment of the park by visitors, and the protection of the park for future generations.

He married his high school sweetheart, Susannah, and together they raised six children, the loves of their lives and his other lasting legacy.

Jack serves on the Anacortes Parks Commission, the Kukutali Preserve Management Board, and assists various community organizations.

He enjoys photography, hiking, being with family and friends, basketball, pickleball, golf, music, writing, flying, kayaking, hot weather, blackberry pie, lilacs, and sunsets.

ABOUT THE EDITORS

Sam Wotipka is a product of the Pacific Northwest. Born and raised in southeast Portland, he has always lived in the shadows of the Cascade Mountain Range.

He attended the University of British Columbia, in Vancouver, B.C. and the University of Oregon in Eugene, Oregon. While in college, his summers were spent working for science departments at Oregon State University in Corvallis, Oregon, growing poplar trees in greenhouses and assisting with botanical research focused on the genetics of corn. His weekends and vacations were usually dedicated to exploring the hidden corners of the Willamette Valley by car or bike or on foot.

For the past two years, he has lived and worked on Whidbey Island at Deception Pass State Park as a member of AmeriCorps, a national service organization.

As a child, Sam's experiences with parks like Deception Pass were limited. His father, Paul, preferred campgrounds and parks managed by the U.S. Forest Service which tended to be free, unstaffed and devoid of other people. It wasn't until the word "Deception" caught his eye in an online database of AmeriCorps positions that the notion of working in a park even occurred to him. During his two years at Deception Pass, Sam has led field trips at the Rosario tide pools, deputized hundreds of junior rangers, coordinated thousands of hours of volunteer labor, created educational signs, and worked a variety of projects interpreting and preserving the park's Civilian Conservation Corps heritage.

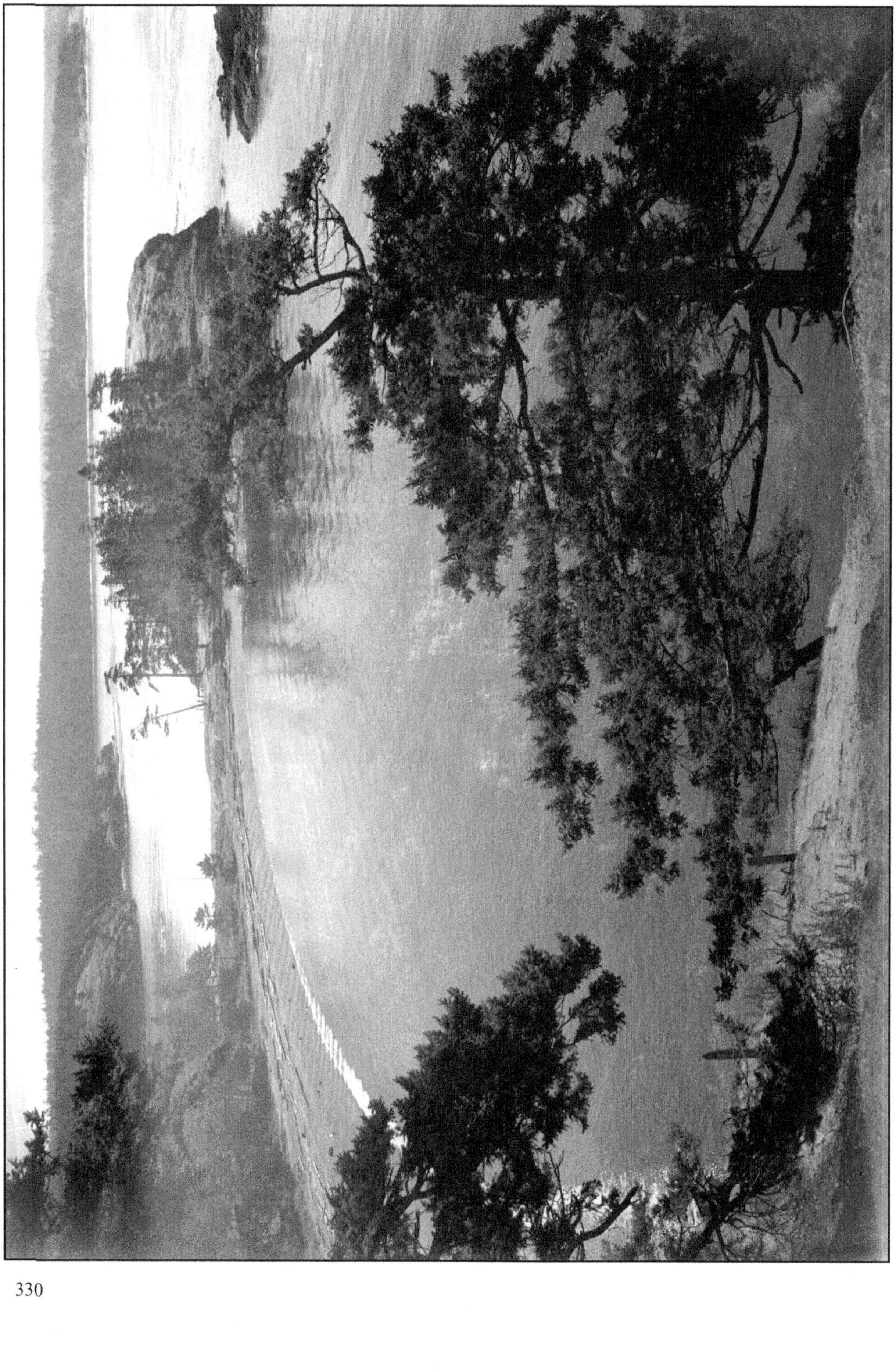